MEL BAY'S COMPLETE MODERN DRUM SET

By Frank Briggs

A recording and a video of the music in this book are now available. The publisher strongly recommends the use of one of these resources along with the text to insure accuracy of interpretation and ease in learning.

DEDICATION

*This book is dedicated to the memory of **Jeff Porcaro** 1954-1992*

PLAY- ALONG Cassette/CD

Recorded Direct to Digital 2 track
February 17 1994 at_____ *Master Control Studio Burbank, California*

Engineers_____ *Scott Sheets & Ace Otten*

Side A With Drums

Side B Without Drums

Tracks

Sketch*
Electric*
Redd Moon*
Home*
FunkyTrack*
Blues Swing*
32 Bar**

*Written by Frank Briggs
*Music Programming & Keyboards - Frank Briggs
** Keyboards - Rich Aronson

Thanks to:

Ace, Scott & Ron at Master Control for all their help and support.

Frank uses :
Noble & Cooley Drums / Paiste Cymbals / Regal Tip Sticks & Attack Heads

CONTENTS

CONTENTS

CONTENTS

FOREWORD _____**By Bob Gatzen**

My first "exposure" to Frank was in the early Eighties...I'm sure he doesn't know this but I went to see him play at a club in Hartford, Connecticut, called The Rocking Horse. His group was called simply 805, and performed original material from an album they had out at the time. I had heard about this great drummer playing this really wild drumset and since I was involved with Simmons (electronic) drums, my interest was peaked. I will never forget walking into the club and seeing and hearing Frank. He was on a huge Simmons SDS 5 Kit supplemented with Roto-Toms and gongs, and was playing "tunes" on the drums by pitching both the 5's and the Rotos. His work was well ahead of its time, and was parallel with Bill Bruford and Terry Bozzio's efforts.

This was the <u>innovative</u> side of Frank....

My next exposure was around 1989.... I asked Frank to perform with me at the Winter NAMM show in Anaheim, California, for the Noble & Cooley Drum Co. We had a sound booth with two drumsets and the idea was to create an attraction so that people would come by to hear the drums. Frank and I met the day before to rehearse. I brought a couple of simple ideas to play, written on half a page of manuscript.... Frank showed up with a musical "score", covering every style imaginable. Rock, funk, Latin, reggae, metric modulation, and odd time. It was an odd time, alright...Frank kept saying, "Bob, it's not that hard, you can do it". Well we did it and did it well...but not without slicing at least 5 years off my life expectancy.

This was the <u>pragmatic</u> side of Frank....

In 1990, we at Noble & Cooley made a decision to sign young, up-and-coming drummers to our endorsee roster. We feel it is important to encourage and support new talent, so we signed three drummers from the West Coast. I have to admit that Frank was the first drummer that came to mind. All three have done quite well over the past three years and we are very proud of them. Frank has managed to be out on tour with the vocal group Atlantic Starr and still compose and play drums for a production house in L.A., teach, and write this book.

Ahh...at last the book.

The coolest thing about this book is that it is for everyone. It is an "encyclopedia" for the drumset. As a teaching method it covers all the essential exercises that develop rhythmic perception and technique. The musical examples cover just about any type of gig a drummer might have to play...progressive rock to Bar Mitzvahs. From boogaloo to songo, for the veteran drummer it serves as a reminder of rhythmic forms and ideas we forget over the years. This is definitely a "drop the needle, or should I say laser" type of book...open any page and something interesting and inspirational will appear. This book is timeless, like Stone's "Stick Control" or Reed's "Syncopation".

Well, that's about it. I just want to say that Frank Briggs comes well-equipped to do work like this, and I am not surprised by the masterful work he has done. In fact, I would have expected no less....

Congratulations and Good Luck,

Bob...

Rudimental Studies

Single & Double Strokes
Paradiddles, Flams & Drags
Applied to the Drumset

Single Stroke Rolls

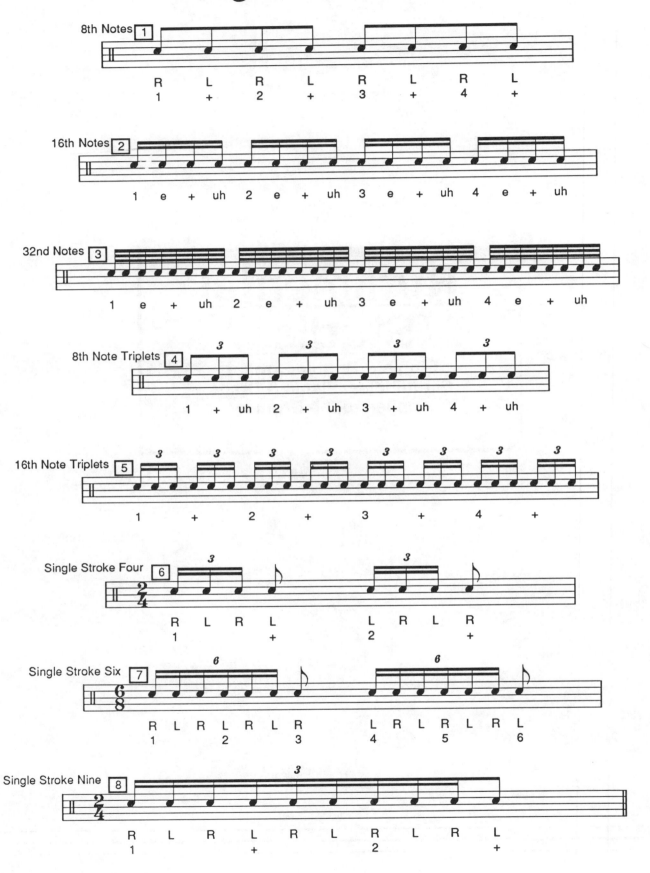

Single Stroke Exercise

Start this exercise at a comfortable tempo and slowly build to your peak tempo.
Play over various ostinato patterns on the bass drum and/or hi hat.

Advanced Single Stroke Exercise

Here is the pyramid of note values in an exercise form.
Use alternate sticking but start each measure with the right hand (or left if you are left handed).
This is a pretty difficult exercise to play correctly, a metronome is a must.
The goal is a smooth transition from one note value to another.
They are presented against a quarter note pulse on the bass drum.

4, 6 & 9 Stroke Singles Around The Drums

Here is a solo of sorts that demonstrates some possible combinations of
4, 6 & 9 stroke singles orchestrated around the drums.
Try practicing 1 bar at a time.

Solo Exercise

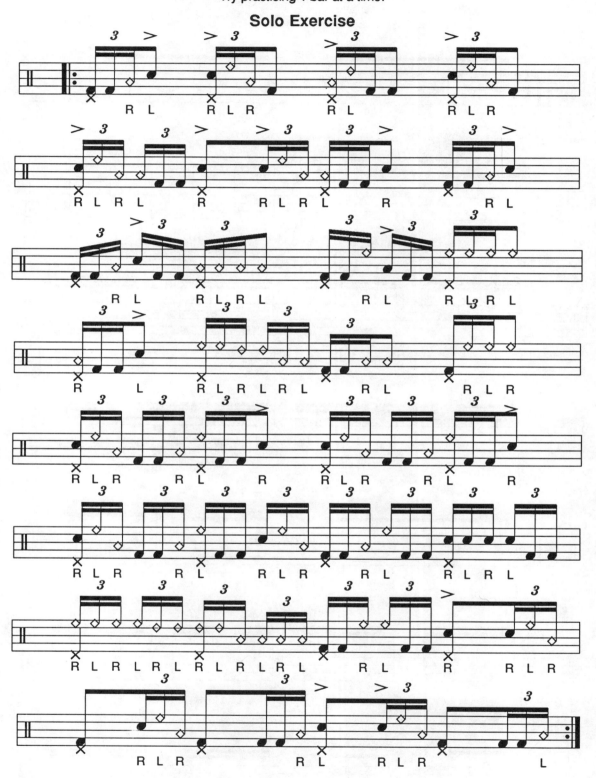

Bass & Snare Exercise

This is a good exercise for hand and foot coordination.
Practice slowly at first, with a metronome.

Double Stroke Rolls

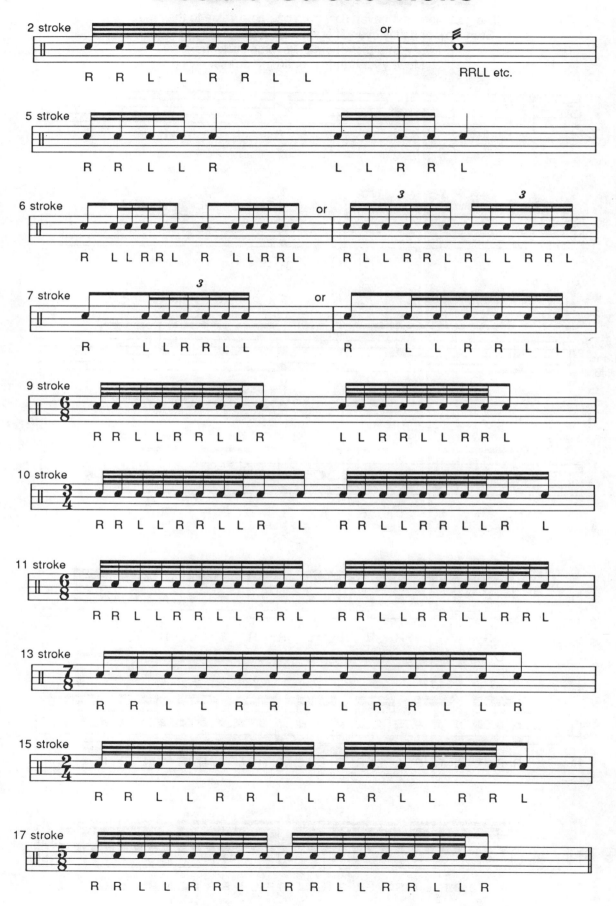

2 Stroke Exercise 1

The goal here is an even flow from one note value to the next.
Start slow and play over different bass drum / hi hat patterns.
Play with a metronome. Reverse stickings.
Move your hands around the drums.

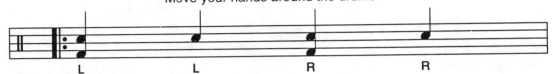

L   L   R   R

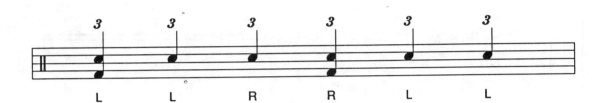

L   L   R   R   L   L

>>>>>>>
Start from
here also.

R   R   L   L   R   R   L   L

R   R   L   L   R   R   L   L   R   R   L   L

R R L L R R L L R R L L R R L L

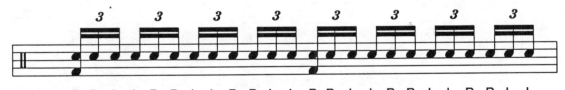

R R L L R R L L R R L L R R L L R R L L R R L L

R R L L R R L L R R L L R R L L R R L L R R L L R R L L R R L L

16

2 Stroke Exercise 2

This exercise incorporates various 2 stroke rolls.
Play it over a 1/4 note pulse on the bass drum and or hi hat.
Try accenting the single strokes or playing the accents on the toms.
Make up your own patterns...Improvise.

Six Stroke Stickings Exercise

This exercise will take you through a few variations of the six stroke roll played as triplets.
Notice how the accents are affected when the roll is turned around
and the stickings used to do so. Play quarter notes on the hi hat.
I use either 2 or 3 single strokes or RLL/LRR to change it up in this lesson.
Experiment. (These work nicely with paradiddle triplets also....)

18

Paradiddle Rudiments

Practice each paradiddle / sticking with a metronome.
The goal is an even flow between the right & left hands.
Experiment with accents.

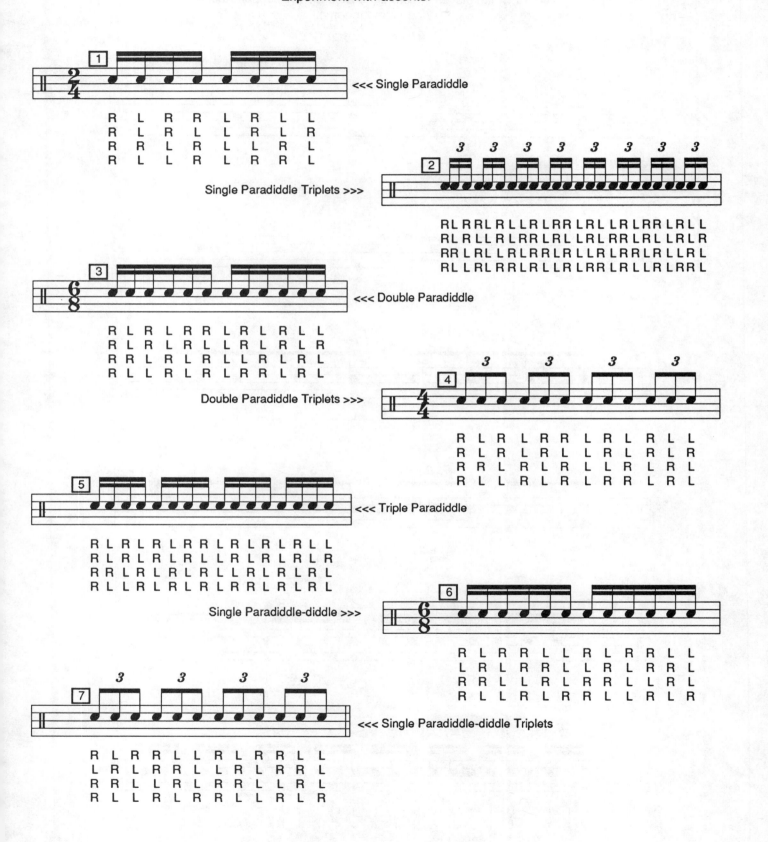

Paradiddle Exercise 1

The goal here is an even flow from one note value to the next.
Start slow and play over different bass drum / hi hat patterns.
Play with a metronome.

Paradiddle Exercise 2

This warmup takes you through all the different stickings of a single paradiddle.
Play this over different bass drum ostinatos.
Practice with a metronome.
Play the accents on the toms or cymbals also...

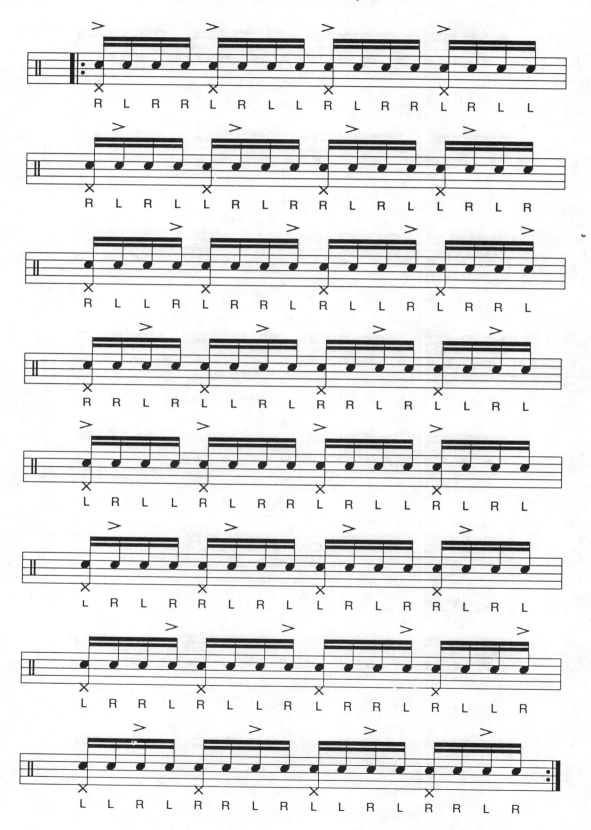

Paradiddle Exercise 3

This exercise takes you through combinations of single, double
& triple paradiddles as well as paradiddle-diddles.
Play over different bass drum & hi hat patterns.
Try reinforcing the accents with the bass drum or bass drum & cymbal punches.

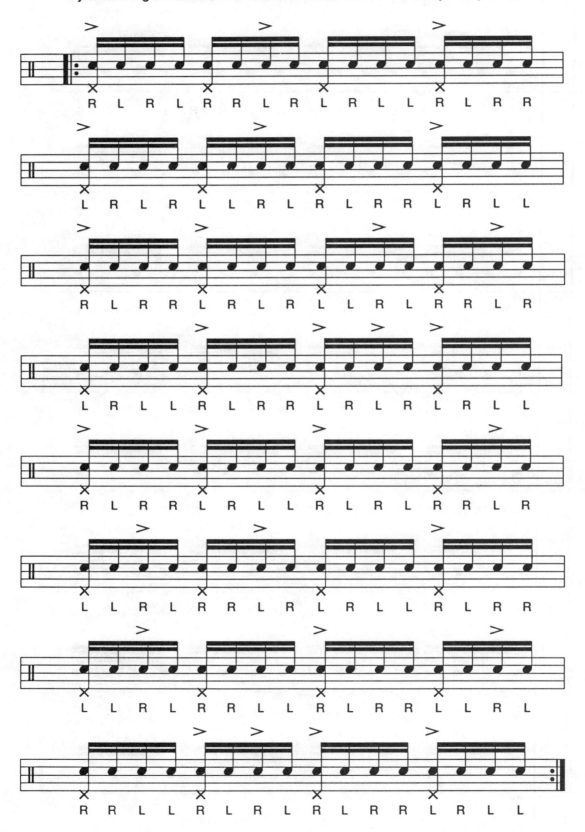

22

Paradiddle Sticking Combinations

These exercises combine different single, double & paradiddle-diddles over
16th and 16th note triplets. Play these with a metronome.
The goal is smooth transitions of note values & stickings.
Try following the right hand with your right foot also.

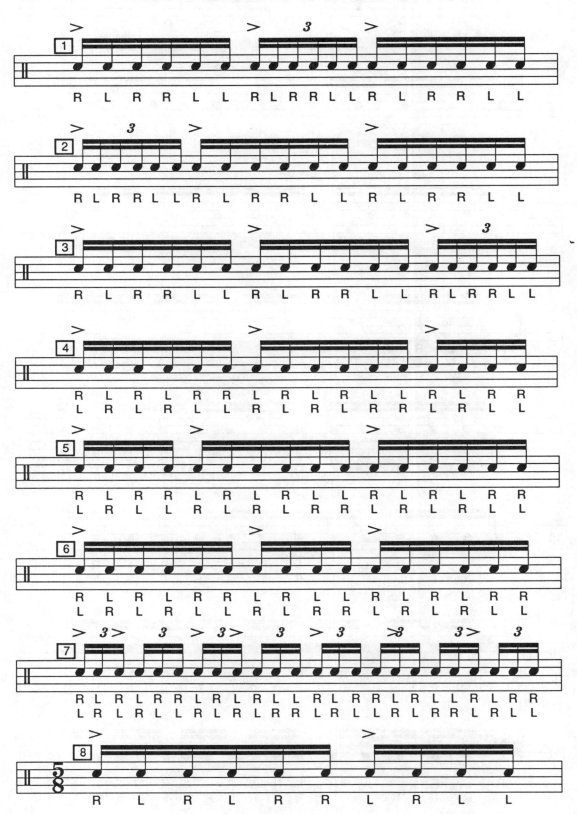

23

Paradiddle Sticking Combinations

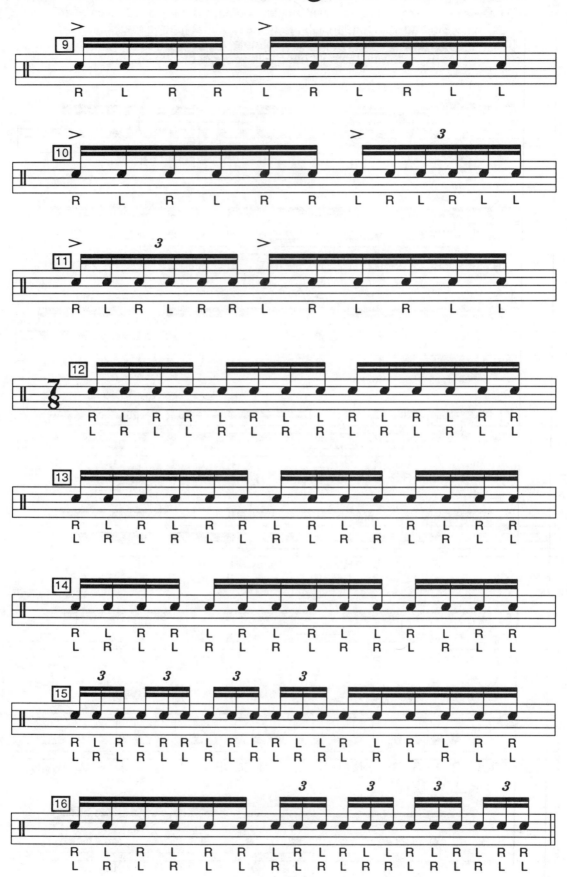

24

Single Paradiddle Groove Patterns

Here are some examples of how the single paradiddle may be used as groove patterns.
All the patterns on this page are based on the 1st inversion of the single paradiddle.
Make up your own patterns using other inversions or combinations of inversions.

25

Double Paradiddle Groove Patterns

Here are some examples of how the double paradiddle may be used for groove patterns.
They are written in straight 16th notes & 8th note triplets, all in 1st inversion.
Make up your own patterns using other inversions or combinations of inversions.

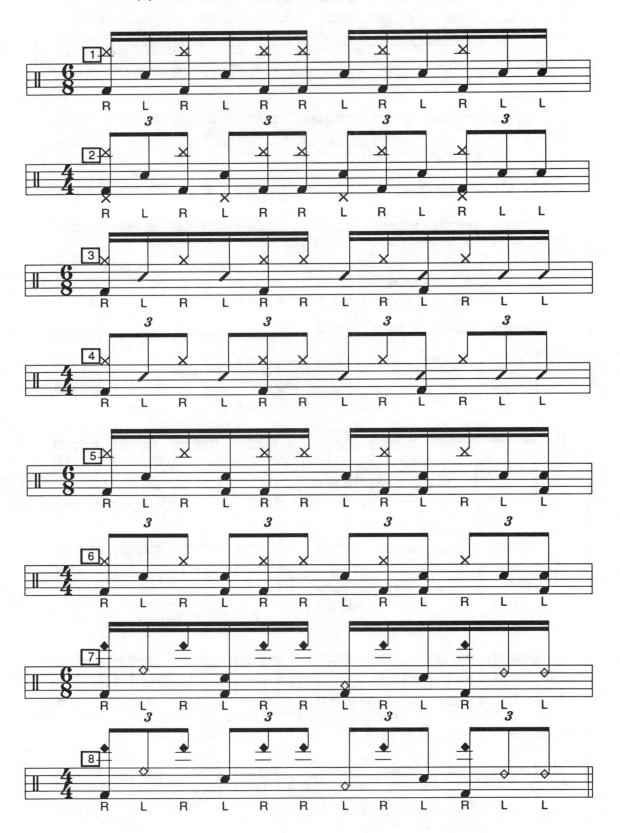

Paradiddle Fill Patterns

In this exercise the paradiddle is presented around the drums. Here are a few possibilities.
Practice one bar at a time, Alternating with 1 bar of time, then connect the whole piece.
Make up your own patterns.

Flam Rudiments

Grace notes should be played softer & closer to the drum than the primary note. When you are comfortable with a pattern try splitting your hands between 2 voices...Experiment.

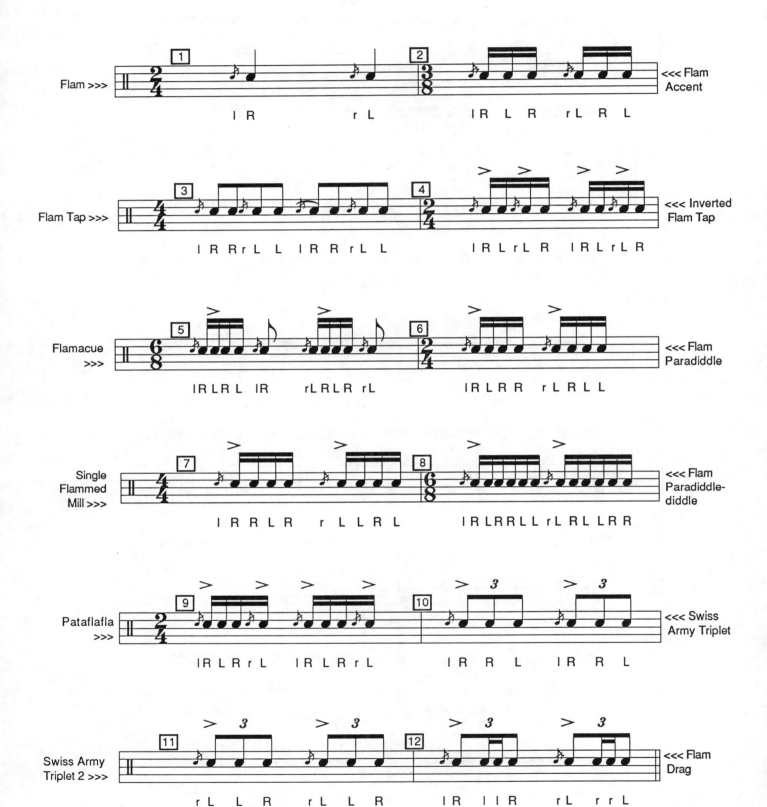

Flam Exercise 1

This exercise will help develop control of alternating flams
by modulating them over different note values.
Start slow and use a metronome.
Play non grace notes on the toms also.

R   L   R   L

R   L   R   L   R   L

R   L   R   L   R   L   R   L

R L R L R L R L R L R L R L R L

R L R L R L R L R L R L R L R L R L R L R L R L

Flam Exercise 2

These exercises will help you gain control of the pataflafla & the swiss army
triplet. Practice over quarter notes on the hi hat with a metronome.
Try playing the non grace notes of the flam on the toms or cymbals also.

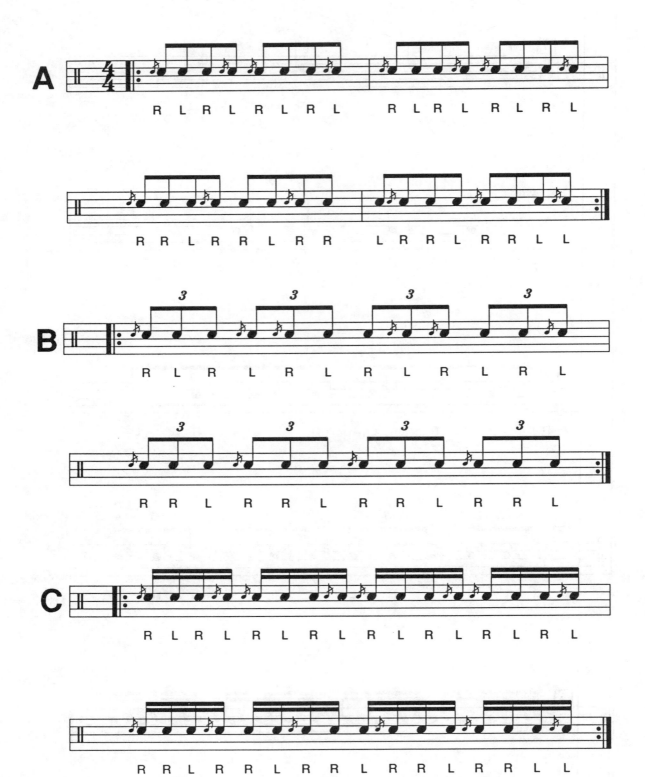

Flam Exercise 3

This exercise will help develop control of the flam tap & flam accent.
Practice over a half note pulse (or other ostinatos) on bass drum and/or hi hat
with a metronome. Play all the primary flammed notes on the toms and cymbals also...

*Play these as 1 or 2 bar patterns also.

*Try splitting your hands between 2 sound sources EX: snare / hi hat or snare / floor tom.

Drag Rudiments

Drag rudiments are probably the most difficult to master.
When you are comfortable with a pattern, play the non grace notes on the toms.

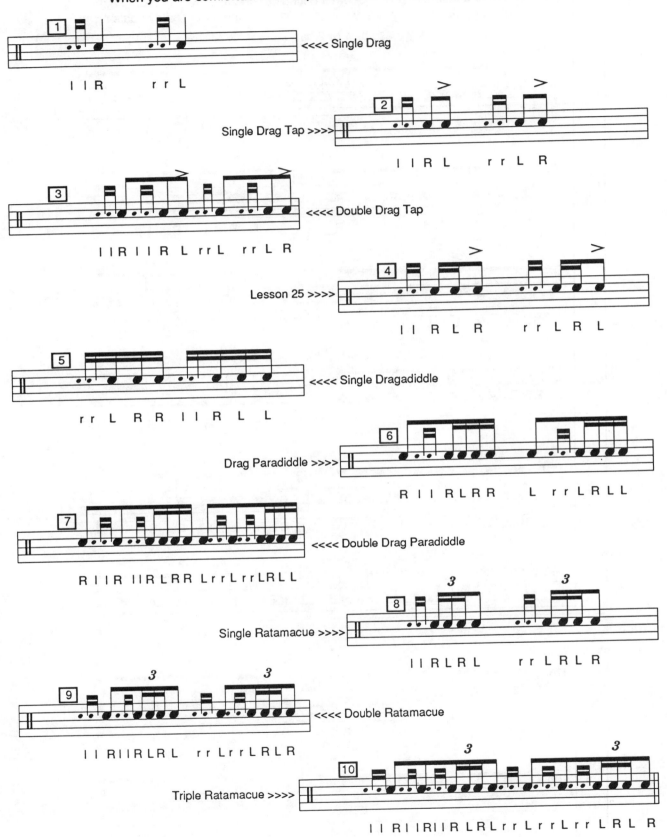

1 <<<< Single Drag

l l R   r r L

2

Single Drag Tap >>>>

l l R L   r r L R

3 <<<< Double Drag Tap

l l R l l R L r r L   r r L R

4

Lesson 25 >>>>

l l R L R   r r L R L

5 <<<< Single Dragadiddle

r r L R R l l R L L

6

Drag Paradiddle >>>>

R l l R L R R   L r r L R L L

7 <<<< Double Drag Paradiddle

R l l R l l R L R R L r r L r r L R L L

8

Single Ratamacue >>>>

l l R L R L   r r L R L R

9 <<<< Double Ratamacue

l l R l l R L R L   r r L r r L R L R

10

Triple Ratamacue >>>>

l l R l l R l l R L R L r r L r r L r r L R L R

32

Linear Patterns

Linear Exercises 1

Linear patterns are patterns where only one voice plays at a time.
Here are some preliminary exercises.
When you are comfortable with them try connecting them into longer phrases.

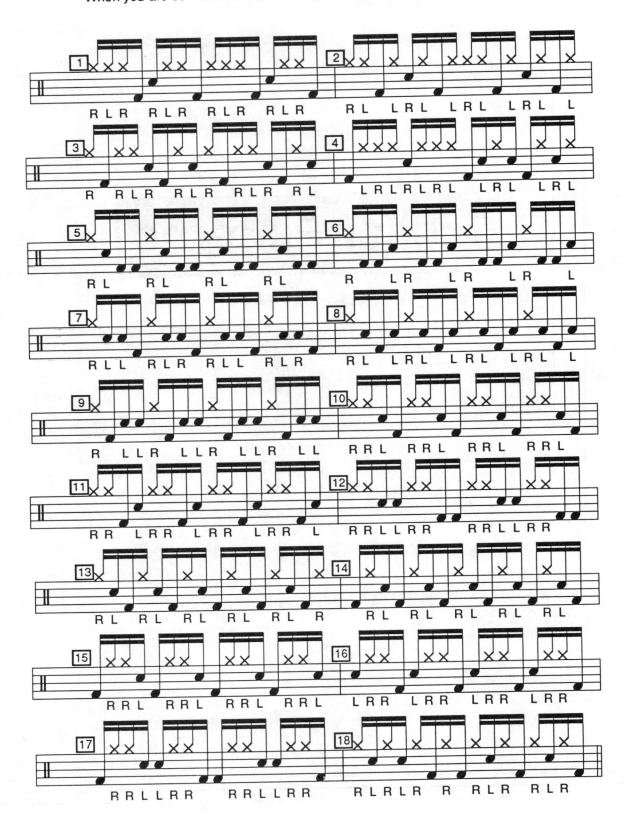

Linear Exercises 2

Here are some exercises voiced over more broken rhythms.
Follow the stickings closely.
The hi hat part may be moved to the toms.

Linear Exercises 3

Here are linear patterns voiced over dotted and sixteenth note triplet rhythms.
The key to the 16th note triplet patterns is hearing the 8th note triplet pulse underneath.

Linear Patterns 1

In this lesson the patterns get a little more complex by mixing and combining the preliminary exercises...

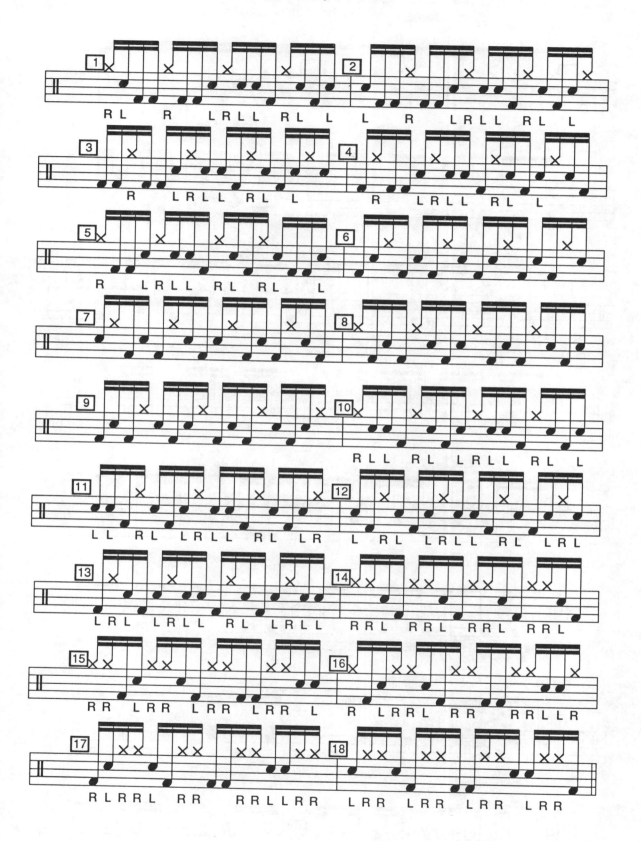

Linear Patterns 2

Here we are mixing and combining broken linear phrases...
With these patterns the right hand is always on the hi hat and the left hand is always
on the snare.

38

Linear Patterns 3

Here is a linear pattern that involves 16th & 16th triplets.
Patterns 2 - 8 are the same pattern displaced by 8th notes...

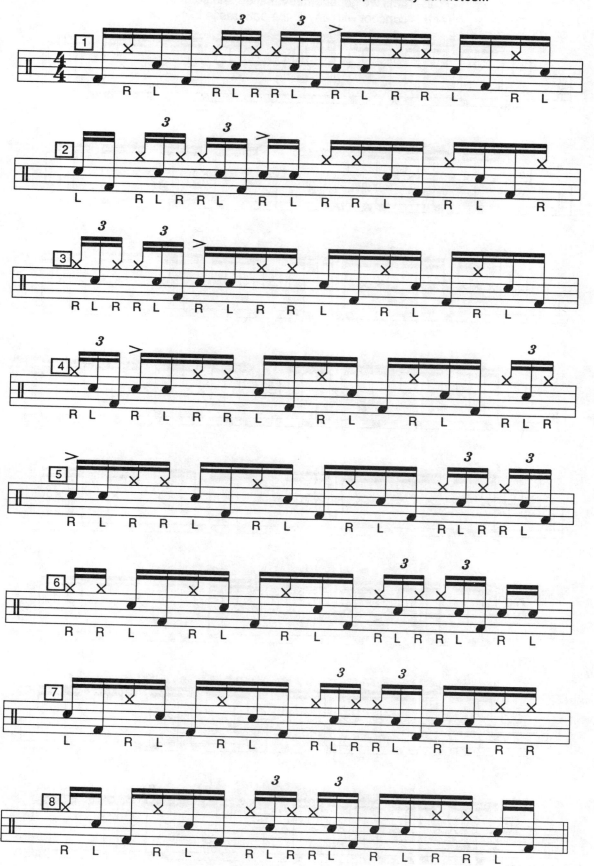

Linear Patterns 4 (Beat Displacement)

By offsetting a pattern 1 - 16th note to the right we get a whole new pattern, displace it
2 - 16ths we get another variation and so on...
Try this concept with any of the patterns in this book.

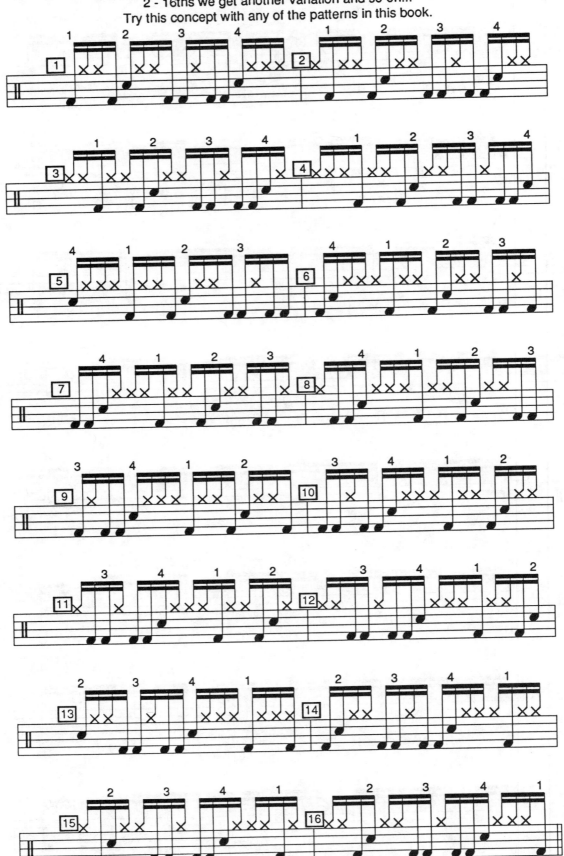

R&B
Funk & Rock

Boogaloo Grooves

The patterns on this page are in the style of the early James Brown drummers:
Clyde Stubblefield, Melvin Parker & John Starks. In my opinion they were the pioneers of
todays linear style and were displacing beats before there was a name for it.
Suggested Listening; James Brown (Greatest Hits CD)
"I Got The Feelin" "Funky Drummer" "I Got You" etc.
and Ziggy Modeliste with the Meters (Rejuvenation CD)

♩=100-135

42

8th & 16th Note Patterns 1

Many tunes were written to this groove (4 quarters on the snare).
Sly & the Family Stone, Martha Reeves, The Supremes, The Rolling Stones etc.
The goal is to develop the ability to play any rhythm on the bass drum
while the hands chop out quarter notes.

Alternate all patterns with pattern 1 then 2, then 3 etc...

Experiment with different hi hat openings & patterns.

Play the snare side stick also for a more jazz / fusion feel.

8th & 16th Note Patterns 2

The focus here is the bass drum against the 1 & uh cymbal pattern.
Jeff Porcaro played this sort of pattern alot.
Suggested listening: "New Frontier" & "The Night Fly" by Donald Fagan (The Night Fly CD)
Jeff Porcaro drums

*Alternate all patterns with pattern 1, then 2, then 3 etc.

8th & 16th Note Patterns 3

Here are more bass & snare variations against the 1 & uh cymbal pattern.
Suggestions:
Play the cymbal part on the ride cymbal also.
Play the snare part as a side stick and
open the hi hat on the quarter notes (see #15).

*Alternate all patterns with pattern 1, then 2, then 3 etc.

45

16th Note Patterns 1

Suggested Listening;
"I Keep Forgetting" by Michael McDonald from the "If Thats What it Takes" CD Jeff Porcaro drums.
"I Will Be Here For You" by Al Jarreau from the "Jarreau" CD Steve Gadd drums. ♩=90-100

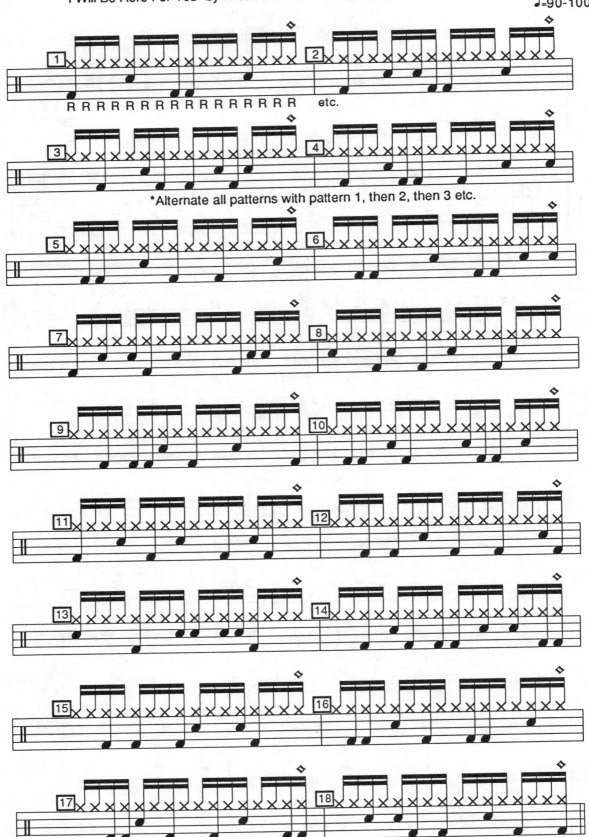

*Alternate all patterns with pattern 1, then 2, then 3 etc.

46

16th Note Patterns 2

Suggested listening:
"Ain't Nobody" by Rufus w/ Chaka Khan
& "Higher Love" by Steve Winwood
John Robinson Drums
Alternate all patterns with pattern 1, then 2, then 3 etc.

*Play the right hand on the ride cymbal accenting the "ands" on the bell
and play all non snare beats on the hi hat for another variation.

*Experiment with hi hat openings & accents.

47

16th Note Patterns 3

Here is a nice variation on 16th note grooves.
Play the left hand on the snare very light so that it blends with the hi hat.

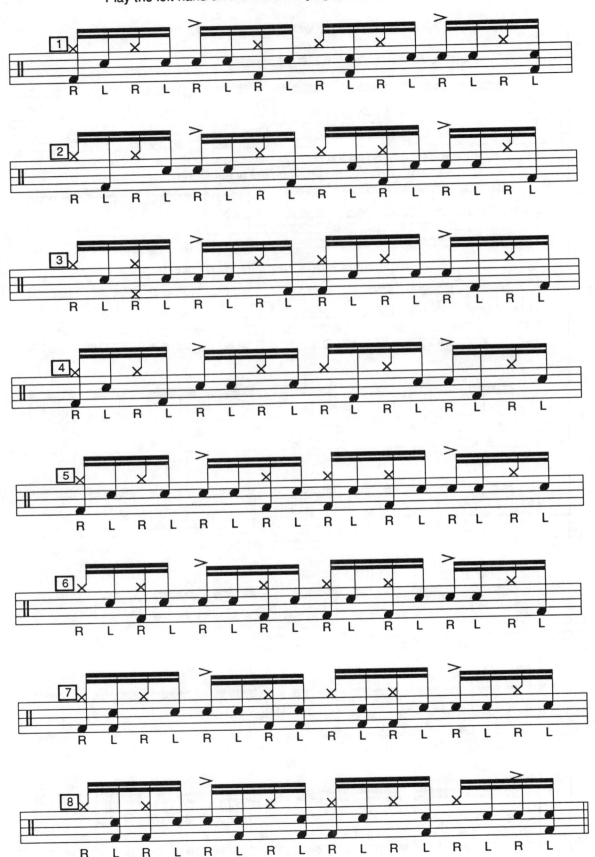

48

16th Note Groove Exercise

In this exercise we are going to systematically move the snare backbeat while keeping a consistant pattern on the bass drum. For our purpose here we are using a 3:2 clave pattern as the ostinato.

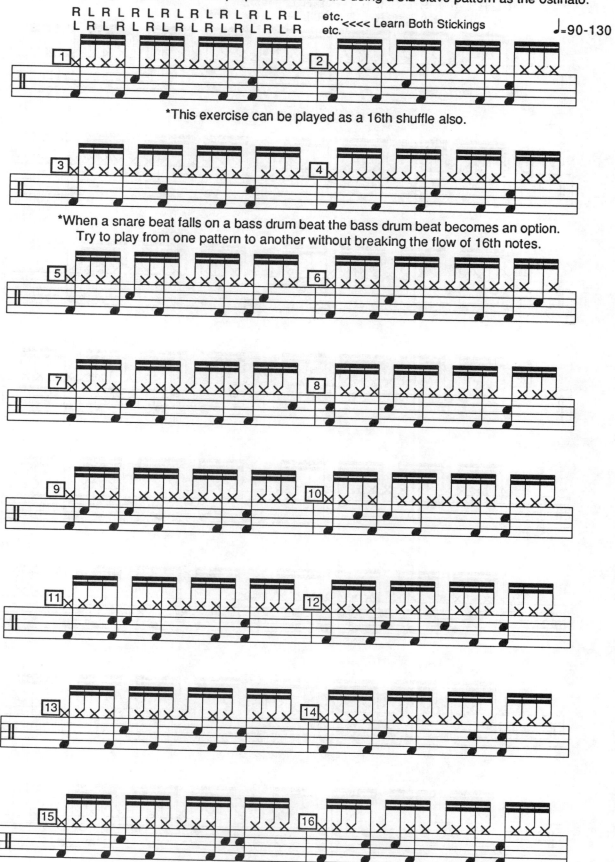

*This exercise can be played as a 16th shuffle also.

*When a snare beat falls on a bass drum beat the bass drum beat becomes an option. Try to play from one pattern to another without breaking the flow of 16th notes.

16th Note Groove Exercise

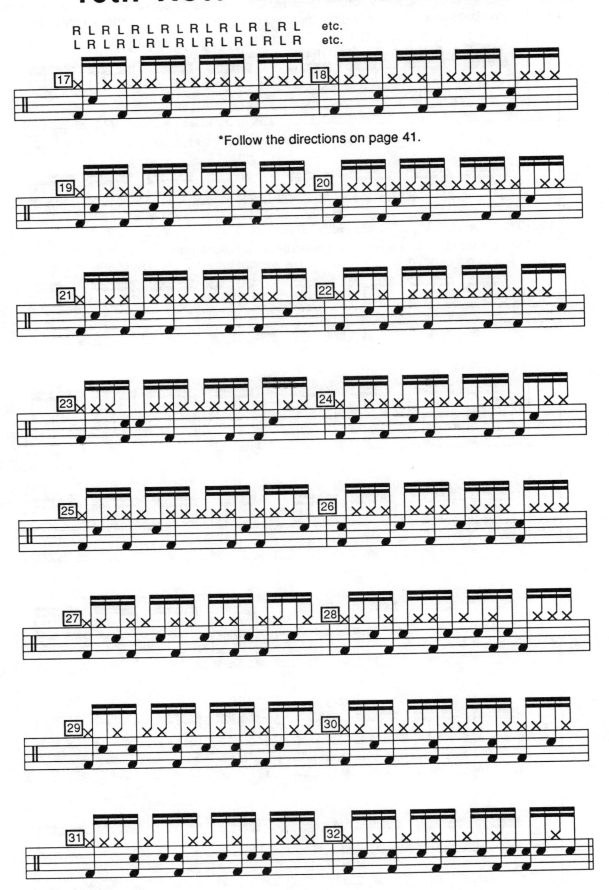

*Follow the directions on page 41.

Adding 32nd Notes 1

One way to embellish a groove is to add 32nd notes. Here are some common 32nd
note rolls and drags on the hi hat. Alternate all patterns with pattern 1.

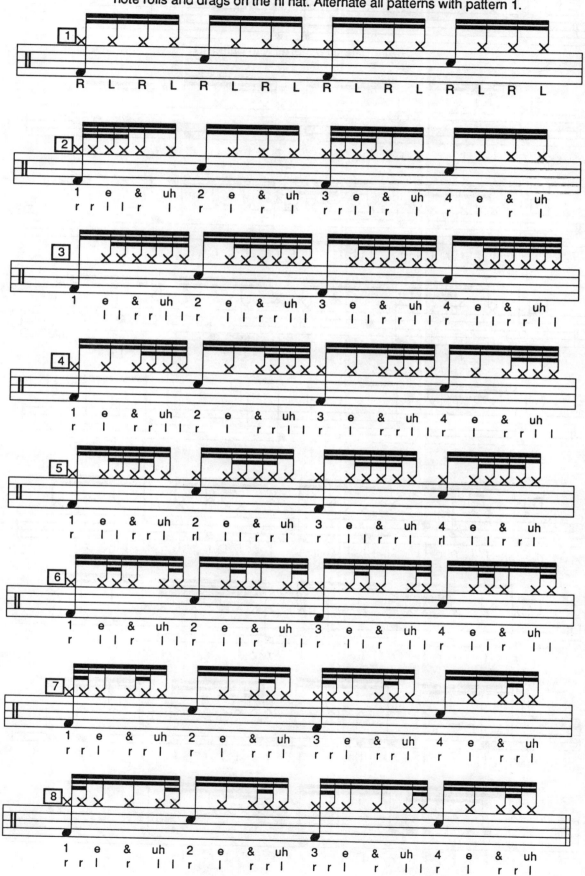

Adding 32nd Notes 2

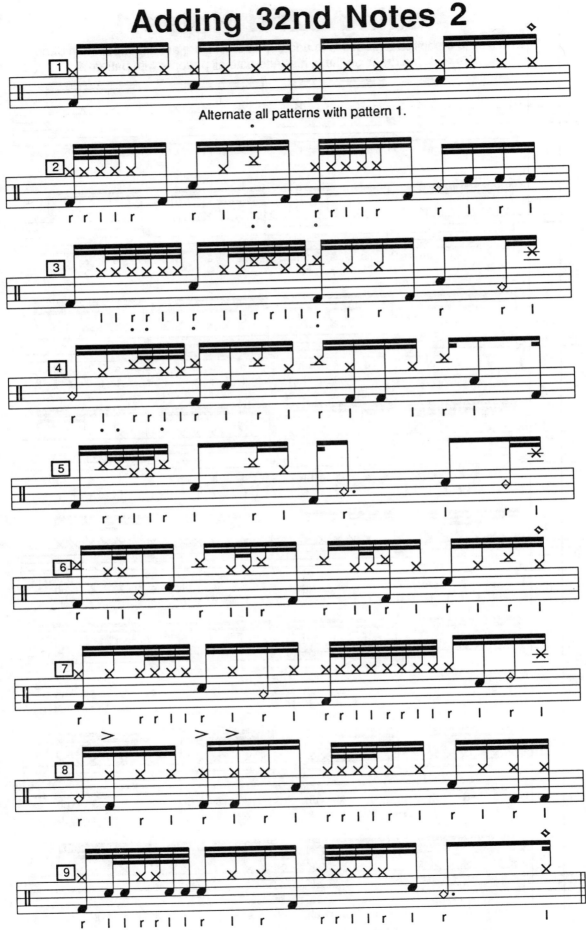

Alternate all patterns with pattern 1.

Blues &
Shuffle Patterns

12/8 Blues Patterns

Suggested Listening:
B.B. King, Albert King, Stevie Ray Vaughan
and James Brown "Please, Please, Please" (Greatest Hits CD)
Donald Fagan "Maxine" (The Night Fly CD)

♩= 50-80

*Use cymbal patterns 1 & 2 as well. Alternate all patterns with pattern 3...

Count >>>> 1 2 3 4 5 6 7 8 9 10 11 12   or   1 2 3 2 2 3 3 2 3 4 2 3

Chicago Blues Shuffle

All snare notes that do not occur on 2 & 4 should be played lightly.

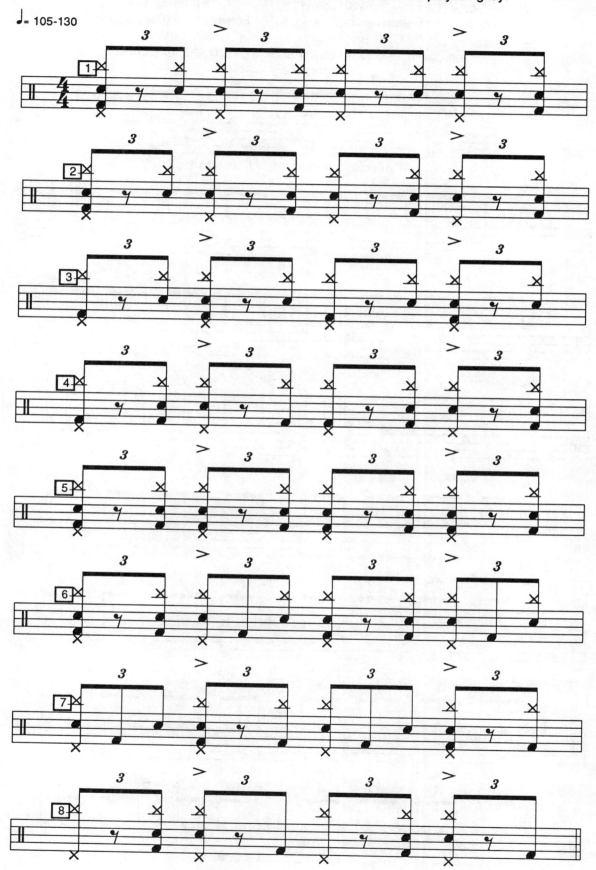

Mid Tempo Shuffle

Suggested Listening:
"Ruby Ruby" by Donald Fagan (The Night Fly) Jeff Porcaro drums.
"Hot Fun in the Summertime" by Sly & The Family Stone (Greatest Hits).
"I'll Go Crazy" by James Brown (Greatest Hits)
The goal here is to maintain the feeling of triplets throughout.
Fills are typically minimal.

*Alternate all patterns with pattern 1...

Mid Tempo Shuffle

Alternate all patterns with pattern 1...

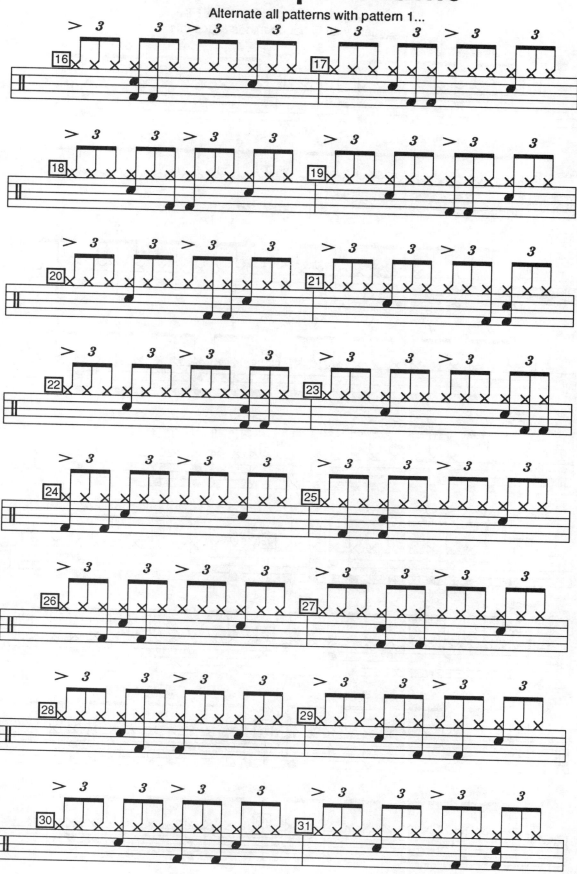

Mid Tempo Shuffle

*Alternate all patterns with pattern 1 &
Experiment with hi hat openings & accents.

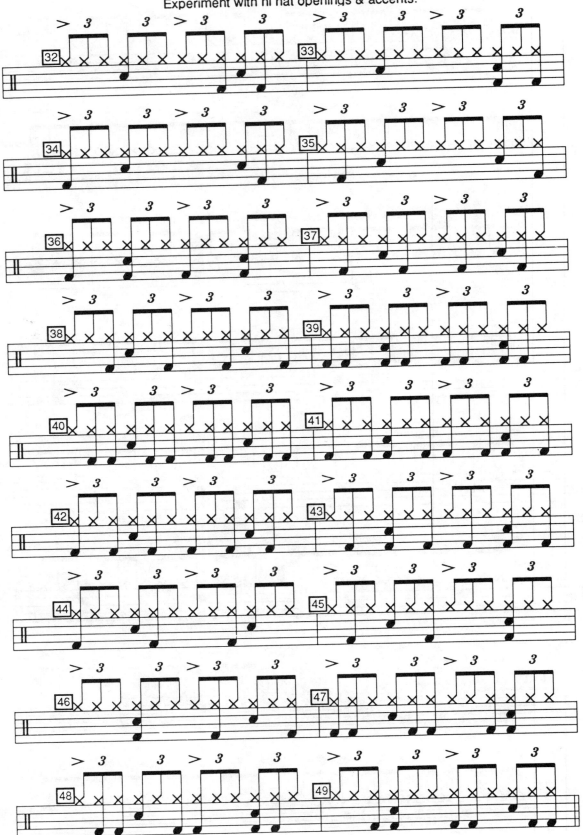

58

Uptempo Shuffle

Alternate all patterns with pattern 1, then 2, then 3 etc...

59

Half Time Shuffle

Suggested Listening:
"Babylon Sisters" (Gaucho CD)
"Home At Last" (The Royal Scam)
by Steely Dan (Bernard Purdie Drums)
"Rosanna" (Toto IV CD)
by Toto (Jeff Porcaro Drums)

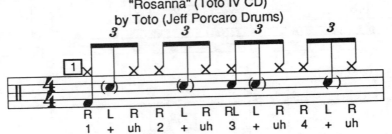

*The ghost stroke on beat 3 + is optional.

*Alternate all the patterns in this lesson with pattern 1...

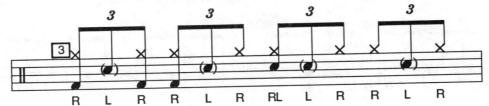

*The ghost strokes on the snare & hi hat should blend as one sound.

*Experiment with hi hat openings and accents...

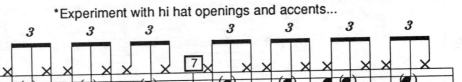

Half Time Shuffle

61

Half Time Shuffle

Second Line

By moving the right hand part of the 1/2 time shuffle to the snare
& playing a 3:2 clave pattern on the bass drum (pattern 1)
we have the beginnings of a style that originates in New Orleans
called "Second Line".

♩ = 125-140

1

Add flams on and around the bass drum pattern.

2

Add a roll or drag before beat one.
Buzz the snare on the flammed notes.
Fill in some of the rests etc...

3

This groove should have a funky march like feel.
Check out the Neville Brothers or Richie Hayward's drumming in the band Little Feat.

4

r l r r   l r   r   l   l r l r   l

r   r l r   r l r   r   l l r r l l

This beat is a New Orleans Funky style.
Experiment with other patterns by playing the cymbal pattern on the snare.

5

R R R   l R R R R L R R R R   l R R R R L

Hip Hop, Jack Swing & Go Go Patterns

Suggested listening:
"If I Ever Lose My Faith" off the "10 Sumner's Tales" CD by Sting
Vinnie Colaiuta Drums
also Janet Jackson's "Rhythm Nation" CD
Alternate all patterns with pattern 1, then 2, then 3 etc...

♩= 95-115

64

Jazz Funk

In this lesson we borrow the jazz ride pattern
and play it on the hi hat Jo Jones style.
Then double the note values and play 2 & 4 on the snare drum.
Alternate all patterns with pattern 1 ex. (1,2,1,3,1,4 etc.)
Experiment with your own variations.

♩= 105-120

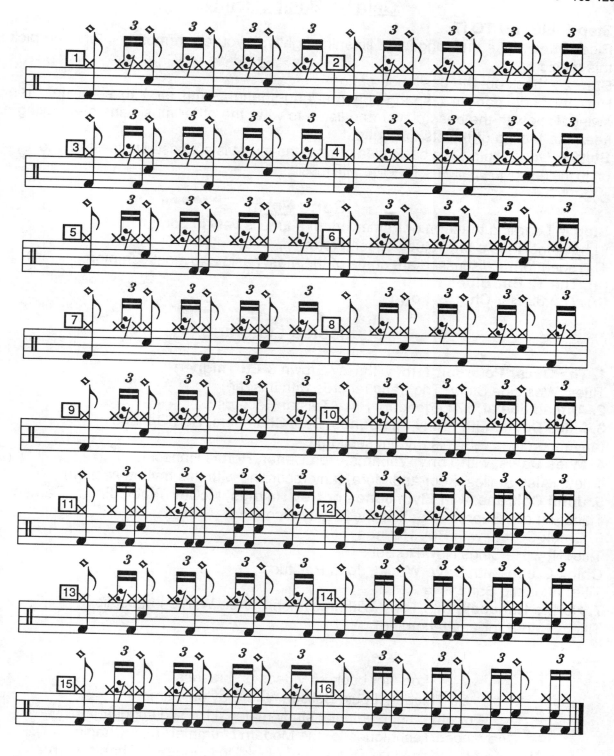

Jazz

This is probably the most difficult chapter to write
because of the complexity of the style and it's improvisational nature.
What follows are some fundimental steps to learning about the jazz style.

Gaining Basic Facility

Step 1 LISTEN TO IT...
Please don't take the suggested listening lightly, if you are remotely interested pick up
this music.
Step 2 Check out the basic ride pattern #1
Play this ride pattern (spang-spang-a-lang-spang-a-lang etc.) to some mid tempo
swing, lock with the bass player and listen to what the other musicians are playing and
keep the feeling of triplets throughout.
Step 3 Once you have a basic idea of what the music is supposed to feel like, move
on to the rest of the patterns. Practice with music...

Song Form

Step 4. Learning the form or framework of a tune is very important.
(I have included a brief study of song form)
The song forms discussed are some of the most basic *and* most common.
(a) The 12 Bar Blues Form
(b) The 32 Bar Chorus Form

Suggested Listening

1. The Oscar Peterson Trio, with Ray Brown & **Ed Thigpen**
Titles: Westside Story, Trio, (any records with this trio)
2. Ahmad Jamal, 17 Legendary Hits / Telstar Records
3. Miles Davis, with **Philly Joe Jones**, Paul Chambers, Red Garland
(any recordings with this rhythm section)
4. Miles Davis, with **Tony Williams**, Ron Carter, Herbie Hancock
Titles: Miles Smiles, Four and More, (any recording with this rhythm section)
5. John Coltrane, with **Elvin Jones or Roy Haynes**, McCoy Tyner, Jimmy Garrison
Titles: A Love Supreme, Selflessness (any recording)
6. Chick Corea, with **Roy Haynes**
Title: Now He Sings Now He Sobs
Chick Corea, with **Dave Weckl**, John Pattitucci
Title: Akoustic Band Live
7. Herbie Hancock, with **Tony Williams**, Ron Carter, Wynton Marsalis
Title: Quartet (or any recording)

Look for books & videos on brushes by
Ed Thigpen, Louie Bellson, and Clayton Cameron.
For other supplemental study material I would suggest
"Advanced Techniques for the Modern Drummer" (Jim Chapin)
"The Art of Modern Jazz Drumming" (Jack DeJohnette & Charlie Perry)
"Studio & Big Band Drumming" (Steve Houghton).

Jazz Patterns

This is the basic ride pattern with 2 & 4 on the hi hat.
The goal here is complete independence between hands & feet while
keeping the feeling of triplets, or swing consistent.
Learn 1 pattern at a time and then alternate.

67

Jazz Patterns

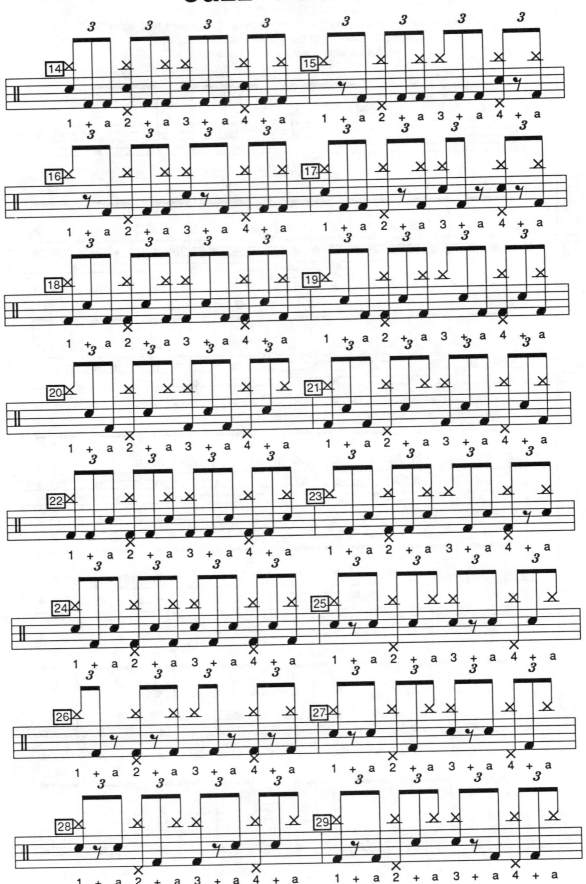

Jazz Patterns

Alternate all Patterns with Pattern 1

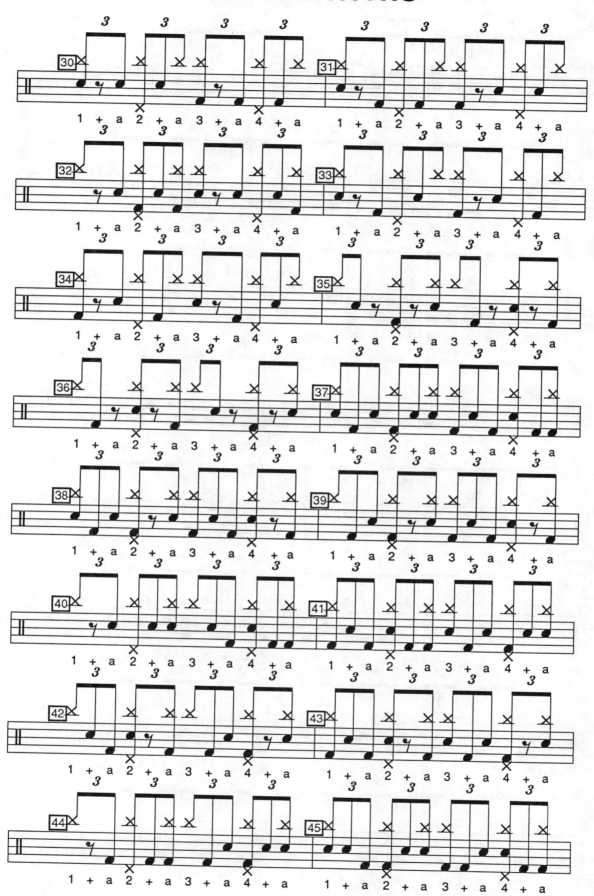

69

Jazz Patterns

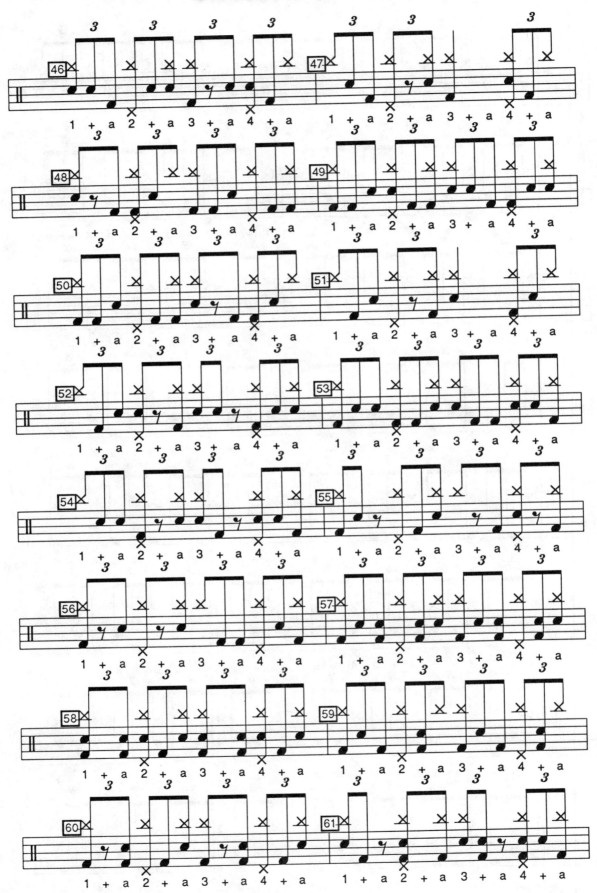

70

Jazz Patterns

Alternate all Patterns with Pattern 1

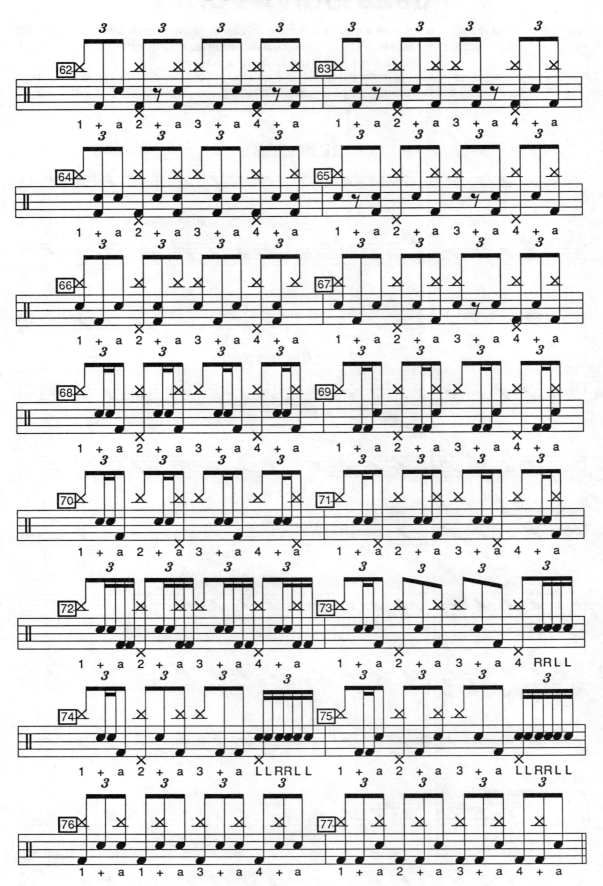

71

Jazz Song Forms

The form or road map of a song is very important for a drummer to know, get familiar with how songs are structured. Here are 2 of the most common jazz song forms
the 12 bar blues & the 32 bar chorus form.
Try practicing in some kind of song form. Hum the melody in your head while you are playing.
There are plenty of examples of these forms and others in the Real Book. Play with music whenever possible...

12 Bar Blues

Example...
Billie's Bounce (Charlie Parker)

32 Bar Chorus Form

Example...
Scrapple from the Apple (Charlie Parker)

72

World Beats

World Beats

This is not a study of traditional Latin, Jamaican, Armenian or Afro Cuban Drumming, but merely an introduction to some of the rhythms of their culture. That is not to say you won't get anything out of the way they are presented here. On the contrary, I believe these rhythms belong in every drummer's vocabulary; whether they are used in a traditional context, or merely used to season other styles. I have found that these rhythms greatly enhance my concept and understanding of rhythm and time, and are alot of fun to play.

Drummers & Percussionists
I would suggest picking up recordings that feature these drummers...

Airto
Alex Acuna
Luis Conte
Tito Puente
Paulino DeCosta
Steve Gadd
Mongo Santamaria
Willie Bobo
Armando Peraza
Johnny Rodriguez
Carlos "Patato" Valdes
Pete Escovedo
Dave Weckl
Sly Dunbar
Mahinda Silva
Olatunj
Trilok Gurtu

Suggested Listening
Look for CD's by these artists...

Airto
Flora Purim
Tito Puente
Michel Camillo
Paquito DeRivera
Santana
Jorge Dalto
Chick Corea
Jobim
Eddie Palmieri
Los Lobos
Bob Marley
Black Uhuru

Clave

The Clave rhythm is the underlying pulse in many styles of music,
it is often called the universal rhythm because of it's use in so many different styles.
It is the the common rhythmic thread that connects much of the music we experience.

3:2 Cuban Clave

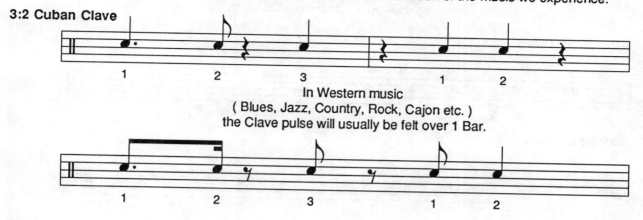

In Western music
(Blues, Jazz, Country, Rock, Cajon etc.)
the Clave pulse will usually be felt over 1 Bar.

Tumbao

A repeated pattern usually on a low pitched drum. Same as Ostinato.

Cascara

Translated "shell"
a pattern played on the side of the timbale

Here is an example of the Cascara over 1 bar.

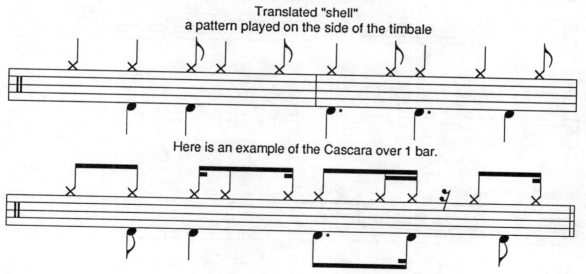

These are a few of the rhythmic components of Latin
and Afro styles of music. There are many different clave, tumbao and bell patterns. The goal of
this section is to help you attain the independence to play them comfortably.

More Clave Rhythms

Here is a variety of clave rhythms.
The clave can be written over 1 or 2 bars.
Try playing these rhythms side stick on the snare against various tumbao and bell patterns.

Independence Exercise

Here is an exercise that allows you to interchange different Tumbao, Clave, Conga and Bell patterns
All parts are written over 1 bar for convenience. You may use any hi hat part that works best for you from column 1
Start by playing all 4 columns together at the top (row 1). Starting at column 2 read down each column one at a time. Move
to row 2; Read down each column one at a time. Move to row 3; etc. etc. etc.
Of course you can pick any combination you would like.

African Patterns 1
The Nanigo

The Nanigo is based on the African clave (see clave).
I have written it here in a triplet feel in 4/4 time
though it can also be written in 6/8.

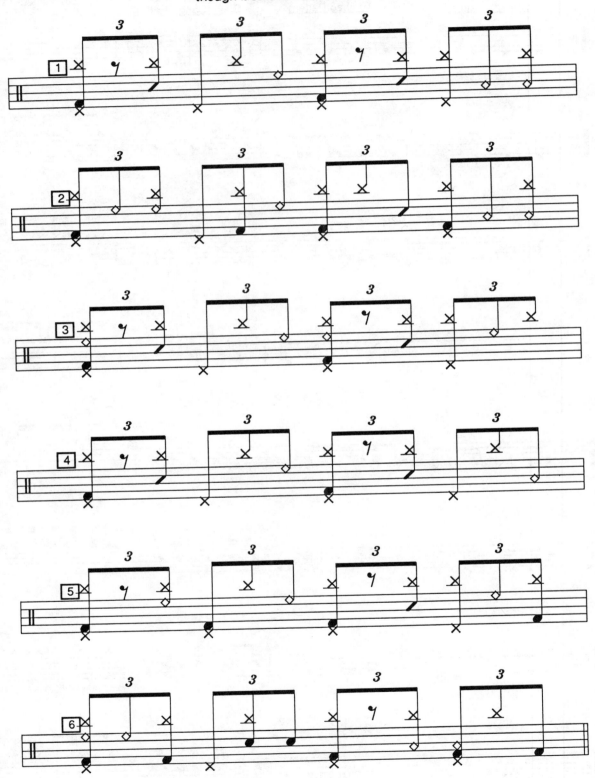

African Patterns 2
Afro-Funk

This style was brought to the mainstream by artists like Peter Gabriel.
Listen to Manu Katche play "In Your Eyes" on the CD "So".
Also Paul Simon's "Graceland" CD and Jon Luc Ponty's "Tchokola" CD.

Listen to Steve Ferrone play "Says" off the Al Jarreau CD "L Is For Lover".
This is a great example of how an African groove may be used in a Pop song.

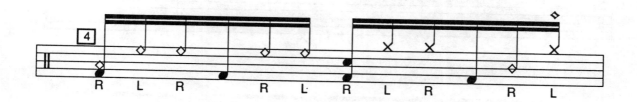

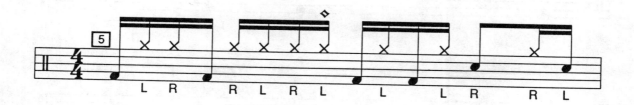

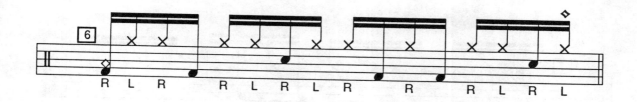

African Patterns 3

Here are more patterns based on the African clave, plus a groove
called the Conga, like most of the Cuban and Brazilian rhythms it was
brought to the western world by African slaves. It appears that we owe
much of our rhythmic heritage to Africa.

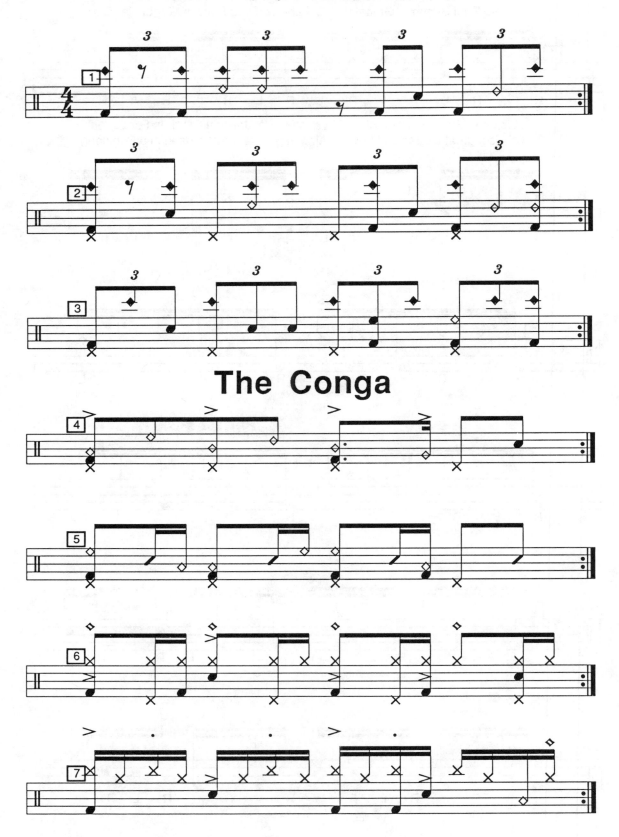

The Conga

Afro Cuban Patterns

Here the Afro Cuban 6/8 pattern is also presented in it's triplet form.
For more patterns of this type see
double paradiddle grooves.
The cowbell part can also be played on the ride bell.

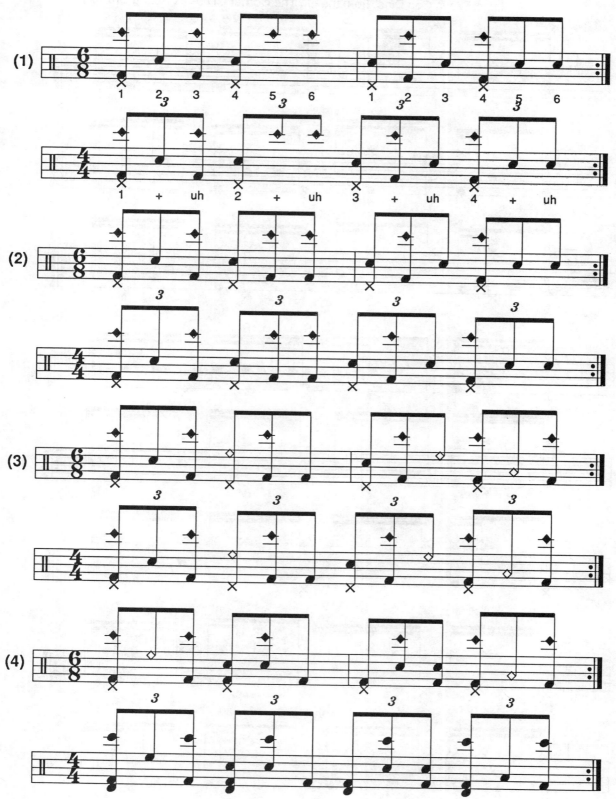

Baion

Another rhythm from Cuba usually played uptempo.
Suggested Listening:
Santana "Soul Sacrifice" (Michael Shrieve Drums)
John Patitucci "Vaya Con Dios" from the On The Corner CD (Alex Acuna Drums.)

$\text{♩} = 115\text{-}150$

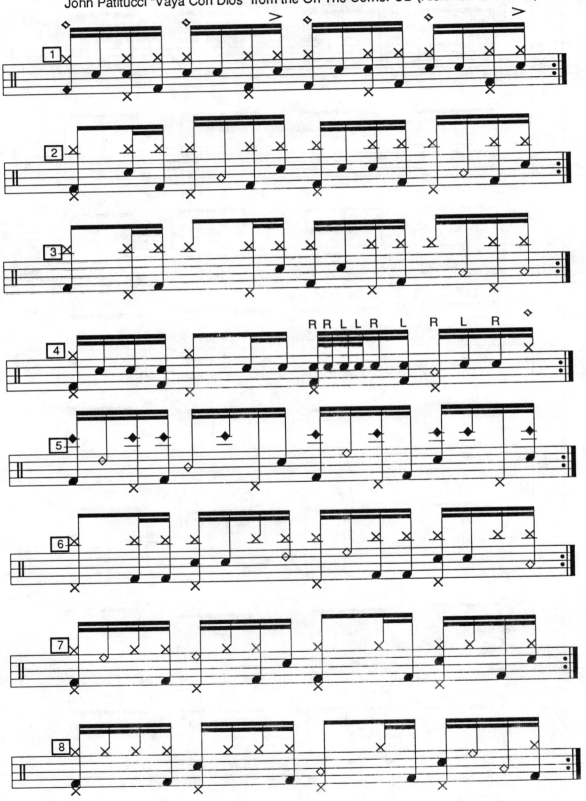

Bossa Nova

The Bossa Nova Clave is a rhythm from Brazil.
Keep the bass drum and cymbal pattern consistant while improvising around the clave with
the left hand. (see Brazilian Clave)

♩=110-170

83

Calypso Patterns

Calypso originates in the Islands of the West Indies.
These patterns are very close in concept to the Soca.

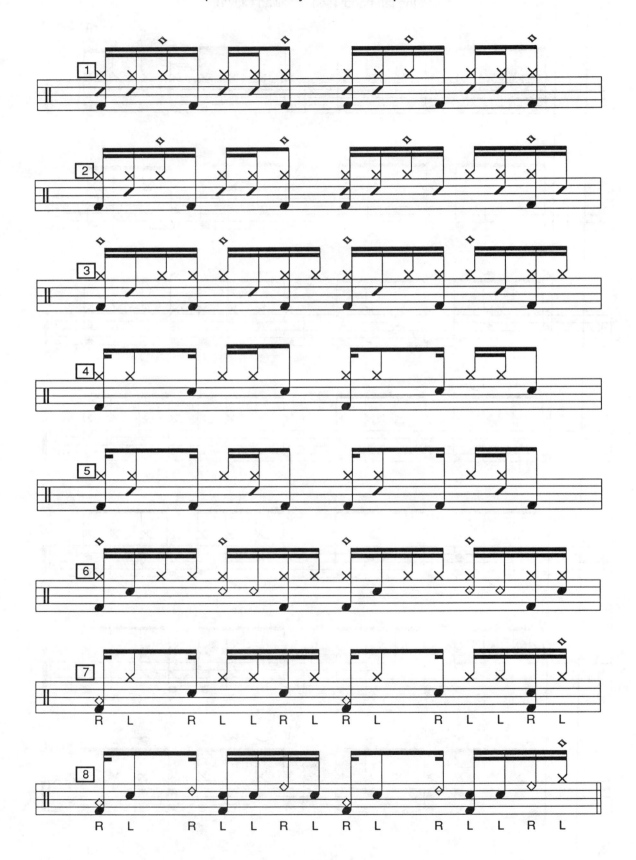

Mambo / Guaracha

Here are 2 South American Rhythms that are very similar.
Mambo can mean a particular rhythm or a song arrangement.
These patterns are a bit westernized. The clave occurs over 1 bar.

Guaguanco

The (gwa-wahn-Koh) is another Cuban rhythm that has African roots.

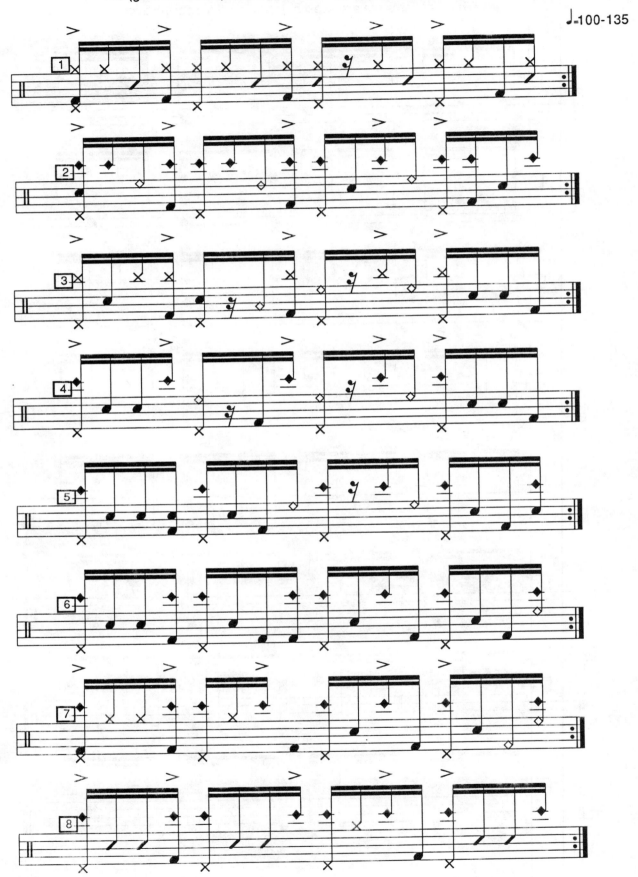

Merengue / Cha Cha / Tango / Bolero / Cumbia / Rhumba

Here are some popular dance rhythms from south of the border

Mozambique

(Moh-zahm-Bee-kay) Originates from the Conga rhythm.
Steve Gadd recorded some great Mozambique grooves during his days
with Chick Corea and Paul Simon and on his instructional videos.

♩= 90-130

Samba

The samba is a Brazilian rhythm closely associated to the Brazilian Carnival and usually played by a drum ensemble.

♩= 80-120

Jamaican Reggae 1

Suggested Listening;
Bob Marley, Aswad, Black Uhuru, The Police & Lloyd Parks.
Drummers to check out; Sly Dunbar, Stewart Copeland (The Police)
and Vinnie Colaiuta w/ Frank Zappa, "Lucille" from the CD Joe's Garage.
Pattern 1 is the basic beat with the bass drum on beat 3, though I have heard some
Jamaican drummers play on the 1 & 3 and other variations.
Alternate all patterns with pattern 1,
or play 3 bars of pattern 1 followed by 1 of the variations.

♩=130-160

Jamaican Reggae 2

Here are some straight 8th & 16th reggae patterns.
By playing quarter notes on the bass drum we have a style called Ska, usually played uptempo.
Listen to Vinnie Colaiuta play "Kingston Blues" on John Patitucci's CD "On the Corner".

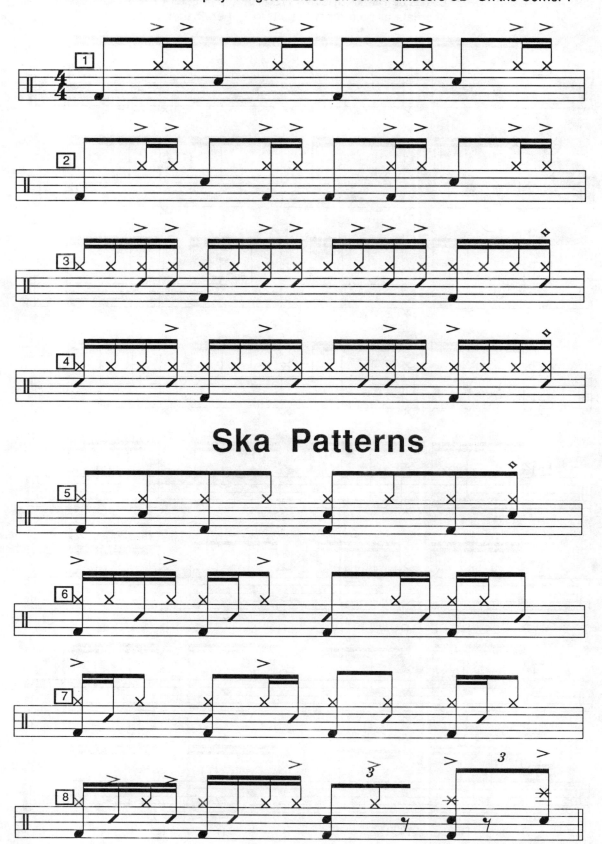

Ska Patterns

91

Songo

Songo is a Cuban drumset pattern based on a 2:3 rhumba clave.
Suggested Listening:
"Festival de Ritmo" by Dave Weckl off the "Master Plan" CD.
Alternate all patterns with pattern 1, then 2, then 3 etc...

♩=105-135

Sri Lankan 6/8

This is a popular dance groove from Sri Lanka (an island country off the coast of India)
Suggested Listening:
"Drums & Music" by Mahinda Silva.

♩=100-130

L R R L R R L R R L R R

L R R L R R L R R L R R

R L L R R L R L L R R L

L R R L L R L R R L L R

R R L R R L R R L R R L

R R L R R L R R L R R L

93

Greek Rhythms

Here are some traditional & very popular
Greek dance rhythms.

Syrto

Kalamantianos

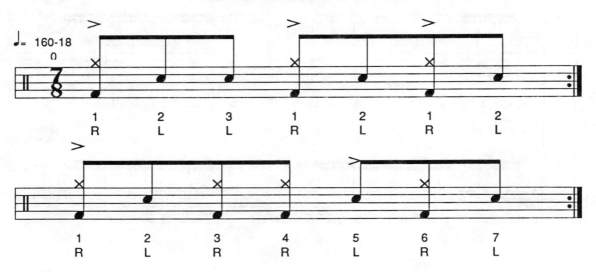

Ziebekeko

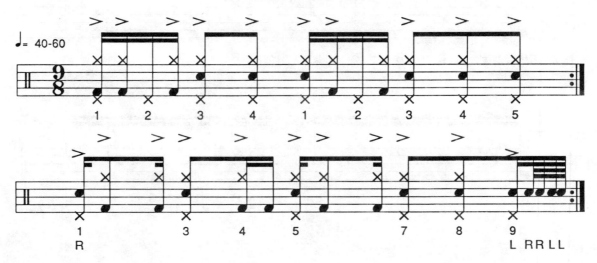

Odd Meters

Converting 4/4 Patterns to Odd Meters

Step 1 >>> (Deletion)
Delete one 16th note at a time from the end of the bar.
Example : 1 bar of 4 / 4 minus one 16th note becomes a bar of 15 / 16.
Minus two 16th's (or one 8th note) it becomes a bar of 14 / 16 (or 7 / 8) etc...

THIS...

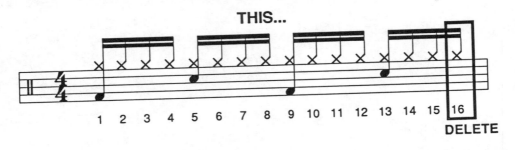

DELETE

BECOMES THIS...

AND SO ON...

DELETE

Step 2 >>> (Addition)
Adding one 16th, quarter, or 8th note, will also change the meter.
Example : 4 / 4 + 1 quarter note = 5 / 4
4 / 4 + 1 / 8th note = 9 / 8

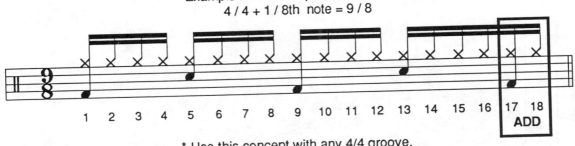

ADD

* Use this concept with any 4/4 groove.
Using 4/4 patterns you are already familiar with is a good way to get a
handle on playing in odd meters.

Improvising in Odd Times

Here is an example of the relationship of 3/2, 3/4, 3/8 & 3/16.
To really gain freedom in an odd meter you must be able to impose one over another.
For example 3/8 can be restricting as far as improvising is concerned.
Try thinking and counting in longer phrases of 3/4 or 3/2 it will open everything up
and give you room to express yourself.
Obviously this concept can be used with any meter including 4/4...

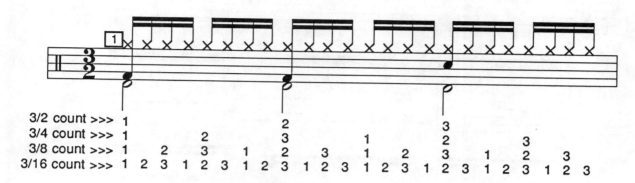

3/2 count >>> 1 2 3
3/4 count >>> 1 2 3 1 2 3
3/8 count >>> 1 2 3 1 2 3 1 2 3
3/16 count >>> 1 2 3 1 2 3 1 2 3 1 2 3 1 2 3 1 2 3

3/4 count >>> 1 2 3
3/8 count >>> 1 2 3 1 2 3
3/16 count >>> 1 2 3 1 2 3 1 2 3

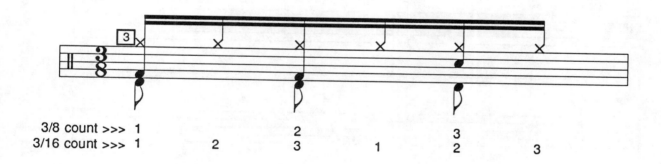

3/8 count >>> 1 2 3
3/16 count >>> 1 2 3 1 2 3

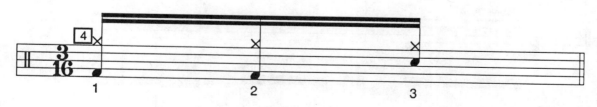

1 2 3

*THE GOAL
To develop the ability to play small 3's within bigger 3's
and big 3's over smaller 3's.

97

3/4 Samba

By deleting a quarter note off a Samba pattern
we get some interesting
mutant variations of this groove.

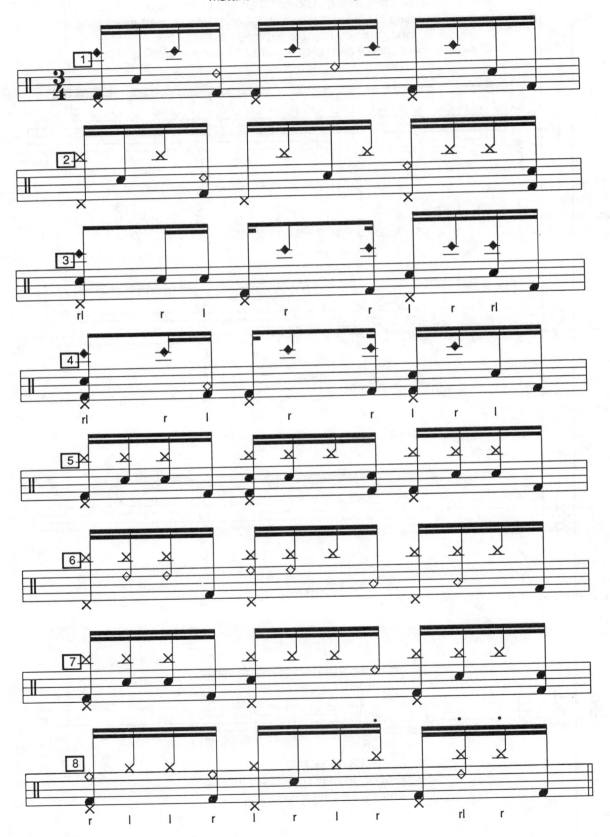

5/4 Mambo

Here we are adding a quarter note to a mambo pattern
to convert it to 5/4.

5/8 Mambo

By chopping 3 eighth notes off a 4/4 pattern we get a new version of it in 5/8.
Here is another mambo mutation...

♩=90-120

100

7/4 Boogaloo

Another way to convert a 4/4 pattern to 7/4 is to repeat the first 3 beats of your 4/4 pattern.
Here are some boogaloo patterns converted to 7/4 using this concept.

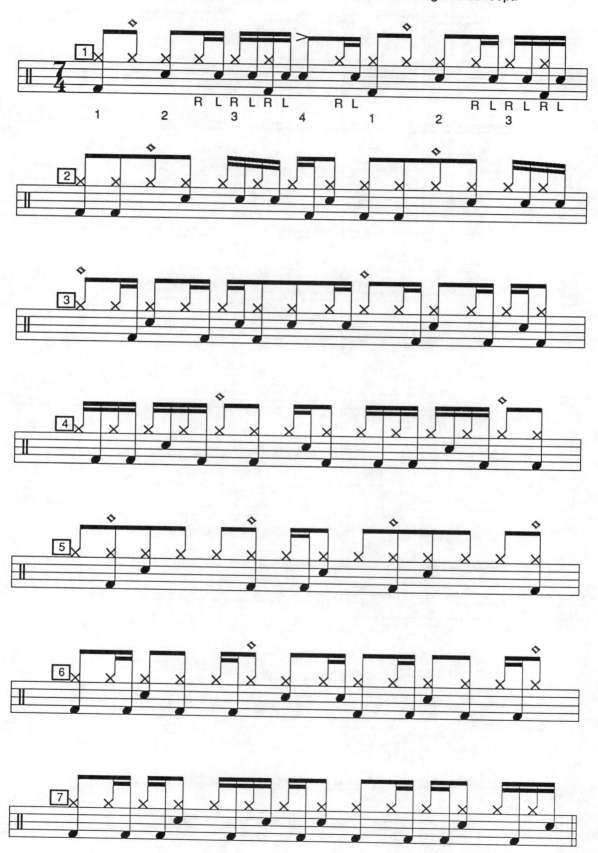

101

7/8 Songo

Here are some 4/4 Songo patterns converted to 7/8 by deleting an 8th note.

♩=105-135

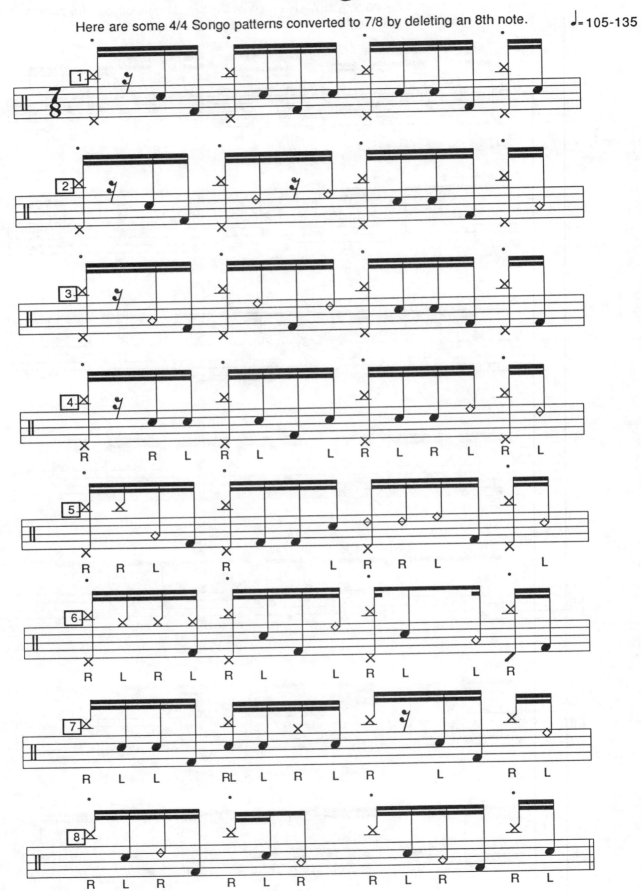

9/8 Linear Patterns

Here is a 4/4 linear pattern converted to 9/8 by adding
an 8th note beat and permutations of the same.

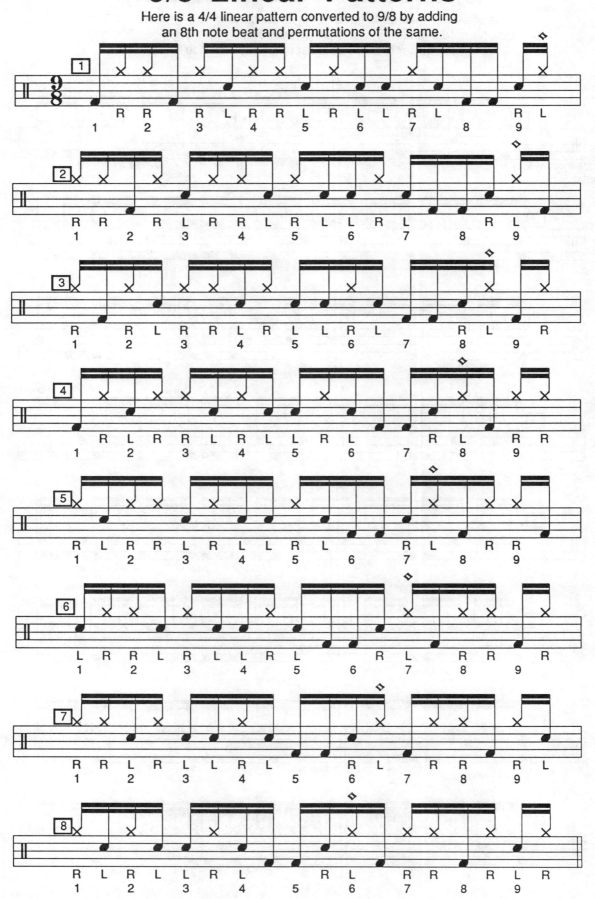

9/4 16th Note Patterns

It is sometimes easier to subdivide a larger quarter note time into smaller quarter note signatures. For example: depending on the groove 9/4 may be easier to count as a bar of 4/4 & 5/4 or vice versa.

Over the Bar

Meter within Meter
Polyrhythm
Fills & Solos
Metric Modulation
& Beat Displacement

Playing 3/16 in 4/4 Time

This is the first step to playing phrases of 3/16 in 4/4 time.
Notice that it takes 3 full bars for the groups of 3 to come to their natural end.
Here are 2 exercises that involve accents in 3/16 over a quarter note ostinato.
Practice the entire exercise. Then practice them as 1 bar exercises and 2 bar exercises.
When playing 2 bars always follow the natural order; 1 followed by 2, 2 by 3, 3 by 1.
Precede the exercise with 1 or 2 bars of time.

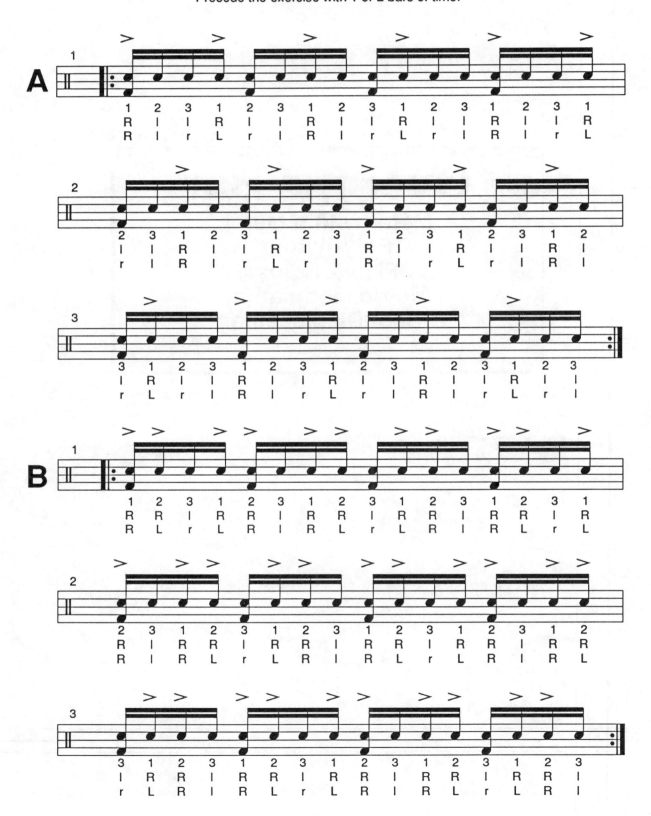

106

Applying 3/16 in 4/4 Time

Here are 2 fill /solo exercises that outline the accents in 3/16 with the cymbals & bass drum.
Follow the stickings closely.
Practice 1 & 2 in their entirety. Then practice them as 1 bar exercises and 2 bar exercises.
When playing 2 bars always follow the natural order; 1 followed by 2, 2 followed by 3, 3 followed by 1.
Precede the exercise with 1 or 2 bars of time.

107

Applying 3/16 in 4/4 Time

Here are a couple of practical ways to apply 3/16 in 4/4 time.
Example 1 outlines 3/16 accents on the hi hat while playing quarters on the bass drum and 3
on the snare. This works well as variations on Ska grooves.
Example 2 modulates the time and creates the illusion of playing a shuffle at a faster
tempo, this can be an interesting improvisational tool.

Try this one with a 2 & 4 backbeat also...

Applying 3/16 in 4/4 Time

Alternate these patterns with 1 or 2 bars of time with a 2 & 4 back beat.
Move the right hand to other voices (ride, cowbell, tom) for more variations.

Applying 3/16 in 4/4 Time

Precede each exercise with 1 or 2 bars of time with a 2 & 4 back beat.
Practice extending all the patterns in this section for 4 or more bars also.

PolyRhythm

POLYRHYTHM - Having two or more different rhythmic pulses
occurring simultaneously in an equal space of time.

THE FORMULA
To Play A against B
Multiply A times B
This is the smallest number that A and B can be divided (A X B = C)
Divide C by B
This will give you B equal groups of A (or the B pulse)
Divide C by A
This gives you the A pulse

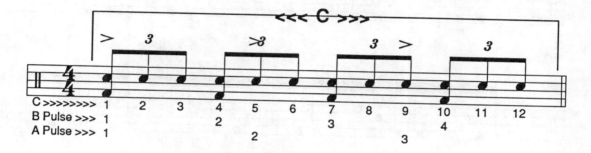

EXAMPLE
To play 3 (A) against 4 (B)
Multiply 3 X 4 =12 (C)
C is the total number of beats in the bar.
Write 12 equal notes in a bar.
Accenting every 3rd note will give you the B pulse.
Accenting every 4th note will give you the A pulse.

*Practice the triplet exercises and
the superimposed metric modulation lesson.

Triplets Phrased in 3

Alternate these patterns with 1 or 2 bars of time with a 2 & 4 back beat.
Move the right & left hands to other voices (ride, cowbell, toms) for more variations.
Try extending the patterns over 4 or more bars also.

Triplet Solo Exercise

This solo combines triplets covered in other parts of the book.
The possibilitys are endless.
Try learning 1 to 4 bars at a time until you can play the whole piece.

*Play quarters or eighths on the hi hat.

113

Playing 5/16 in 4/4 Time

This is the first step to playing phrases of 5/16 in 4/4 time.
It takes 5 full bars for the groups of 5 to come to their natural end.
Here are 2 exercises that involve different accents in 5/16 over a quarter note ostinato.
Practice the entire exercise, then break it up into 1 & 2 bar exercises.
When playing 2 bars always follow the natural order; bar 1 followed by 2, 2 by 3, 5 by 1
etc. so as not to break the groups of 5.

Playing 5/16 in 4/4 Time

Here is an exercise that involves accents in 5/16 over a samba ostinato.
When you are comfortable with this play the accents on a cowbell or on the toms.
Practice the entire exercise, then break it up into 1 & 2 bar exercises.
When playing 2 bars always follow the natural order; bar 1 followed by 2, 2 by 3, 5 by 1
etc. so as not to break the groups of 5.

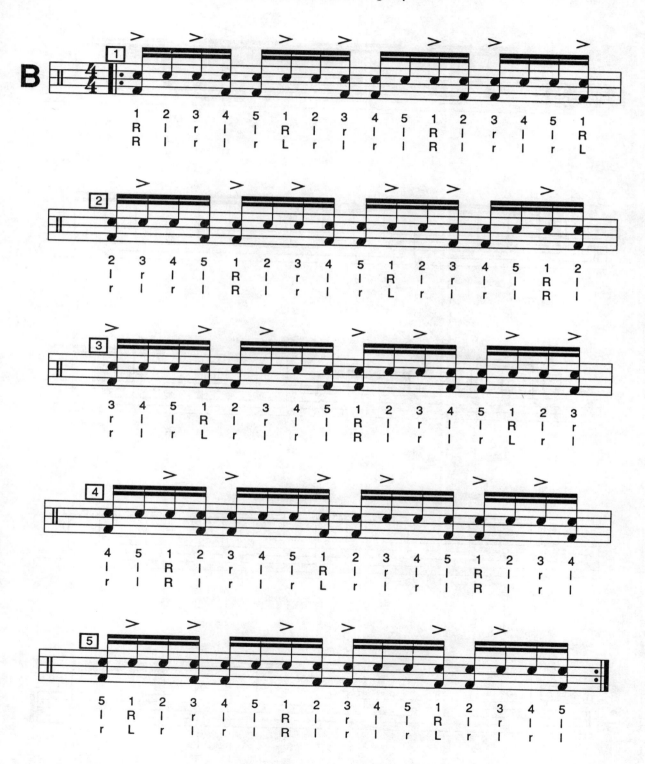

115

Applying 5/16 in 4/4 Time

Here are 2 fill / solo exercises that outline accents in 5/16 with the cymbals & bass drum.
Follow the stickings closely. Try filling the notes between accents with toms.
Practice the entire exercise, then break it up into 1 & 2 bar exercises.
When playing 2 bars always follow the natural order; bar 1 followed by 2, 2 by 3, 5 by 1 etc.
so as not to break the groups of 5. Precede with 1 or 2 bars of time.

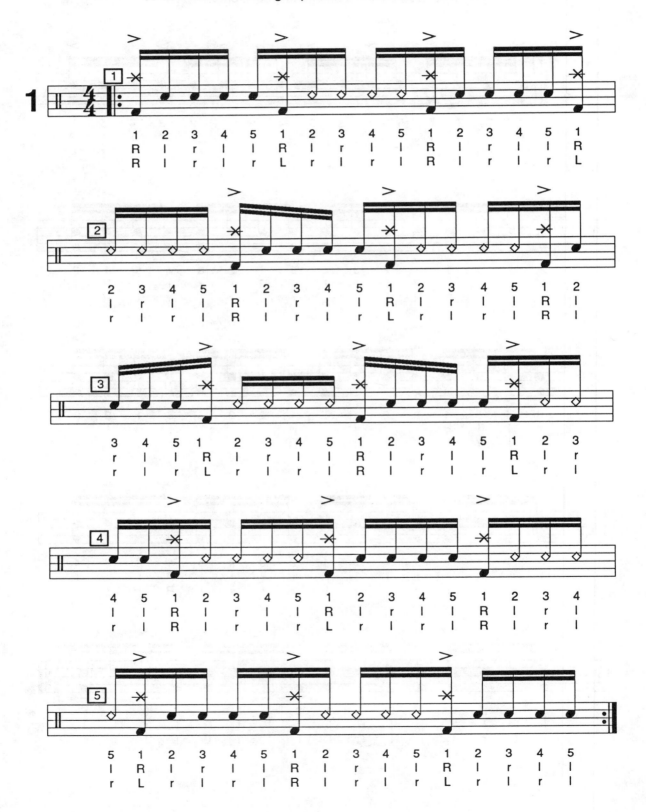

116

Applying 5/16 in 4/4 Time

This exercise outlines accents in 5/16 with the cymbals and bass drum. Follow the stickings closely. Try playing the unaccented notes on combinations of snare & toms.

Practice the entire exercise, then break it up into 1 and 2 bar phrases.

117

Applying 5/16 in 4/4 Time

Here is an exercise that involves accents in 5/16 over a samba ostinato.
Play the hi hat part on a cowbell or ride cymbal also.
When you are comfortable with this reverse the sticking and play the left hand on the hi hat.
Practice the entire exercise, then break it up into 1 & 2 bar exercises.
When playing 2 bars always follow the natural order; bar 1 followed by 2, 2 by 3, 5 by 1
etc. so as not to break the groups of 5.

3

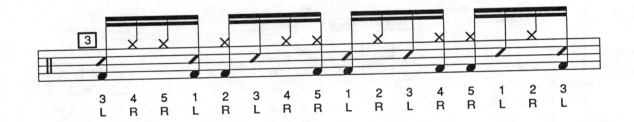

Applying 5/16 in 4/4 Time

In this exercise we are literally imposing a 5/16 time pattern over 4/4.
Alternate between these and a time pattern that accents 2 & 4.
Play in 2 & 4 bar phrases and practice extending the phrases 4 bars & beyond.

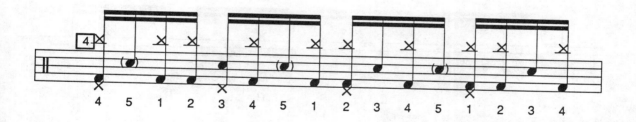

119

Applying 5/16 in 4/4 Time

Follow the directions in the previous 5/16 lessons.
Play 1 or 2 bars of time before each exercise.
Move your right and left hand around the drums for more variations.

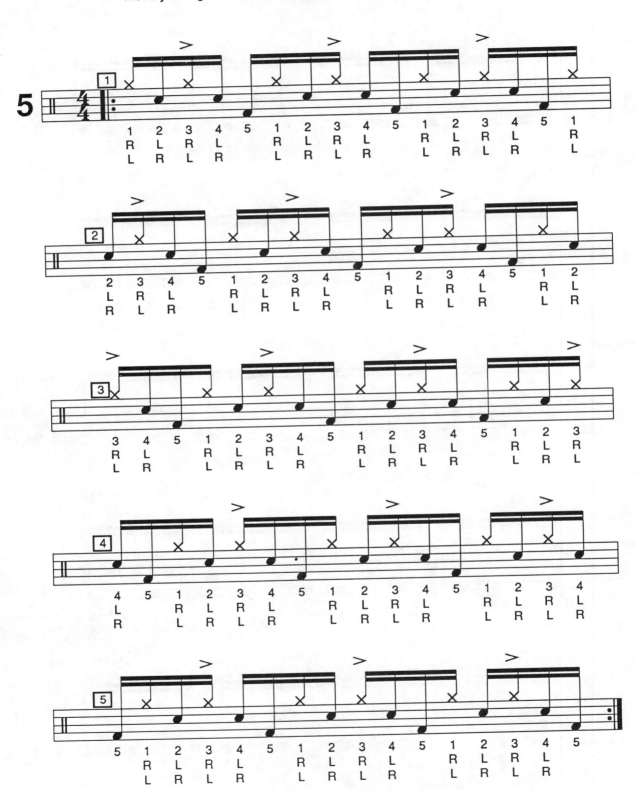

PolyRhythm

POLYRHYTHM - Having two or more different rhythmic pulses occurring simultaneously in an equal space of time.

THE FORMULA
To Play A against B
Multiply A times B
This is the smallest number that A and B can be divided (A X B = C)
Divide C by B
This will give you B equal groups of A (or the B pulse)
Divide C by A
This gives you the A pulse

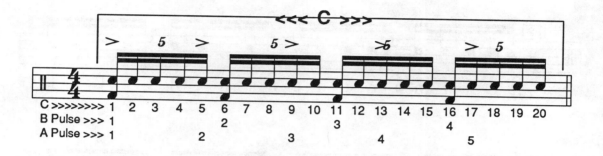

EXAMPLE
To play 5 (A) against 4 (B)
Multiply 5 X 4 = 20 (C)
C is the total number of beats in the bar.
Write 20 equal notes in a bar.
Accenting every 5th note gives you the B pulse.
Accenting every 4th note gives you the A pulse.

*Practice the Quintuplet exercises...

121

Quintuplets

A group of 5 equal notes to be played in the time of 4 of the same kind, in the regular rhythm.
Example: 5 -16th notes that occur in the space of 1/4 note, or 4 -16th notes in 4/4 time.
Here are some stickings and fill patterns.
Practice slowly until you can hear & feel the 5 subdivision.
Play 1 or 3 bars of time before each pattern.

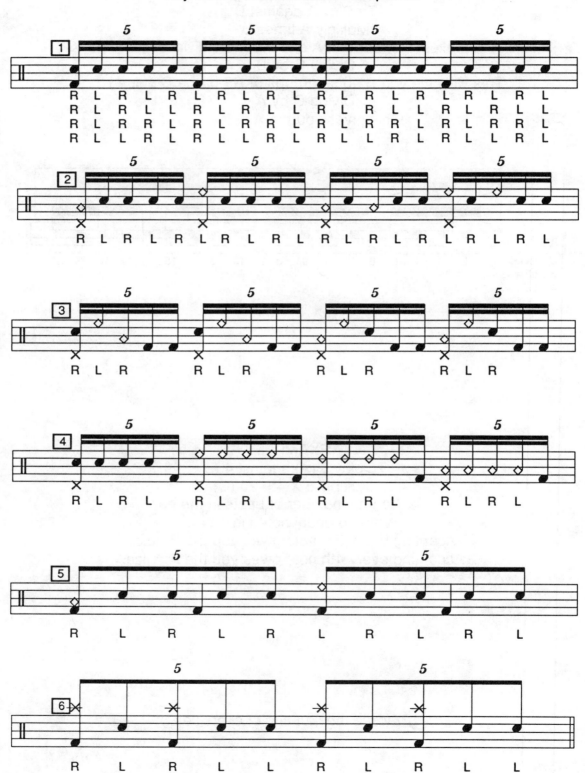

Playing 7/16 in 4/4 Time

This is the first step to playing 7/16 in 4/4 time.
It takes 7 full bars for the groups of 7 to come to their natural end.
Here are 2 exercises that involve different accents in 7/16 over a quarter note ostinato.

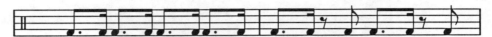

Play the exercises over these ostinato figures also.

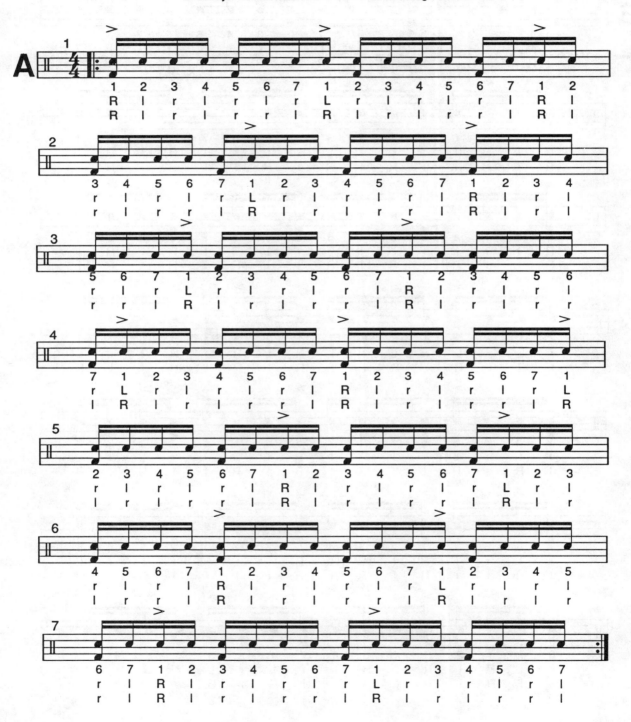

123

Playing 7/16 in 4/4 Time

Practice the entire exercise, then break A & B up into 1 & 2 bar exercises.
When playing 2 or more bars always follow the natural order of bars,
(bar 1 followed by 2, 2 by 3, 7 by 1 etc.)
so as not to break up the groups of 7.

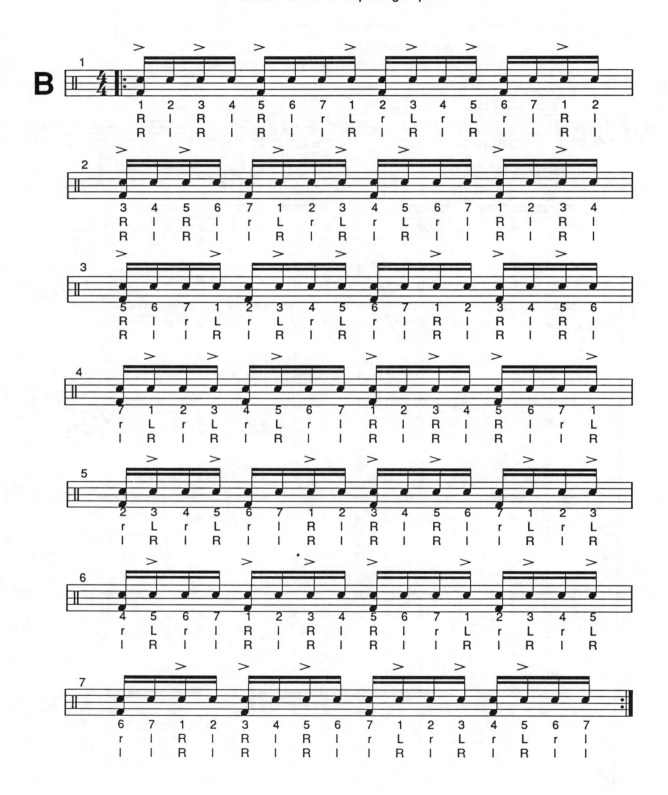

Applying 7/16 in 4/4 Time

Fill/Solo Patterns

Practice the entire exercise, then break it up into 1 & 2 bar exercises.
When playing 2 or more bars always follow the natural order of bars. Precede by 1 or 2 bars of
time. Follow the stickings closely.

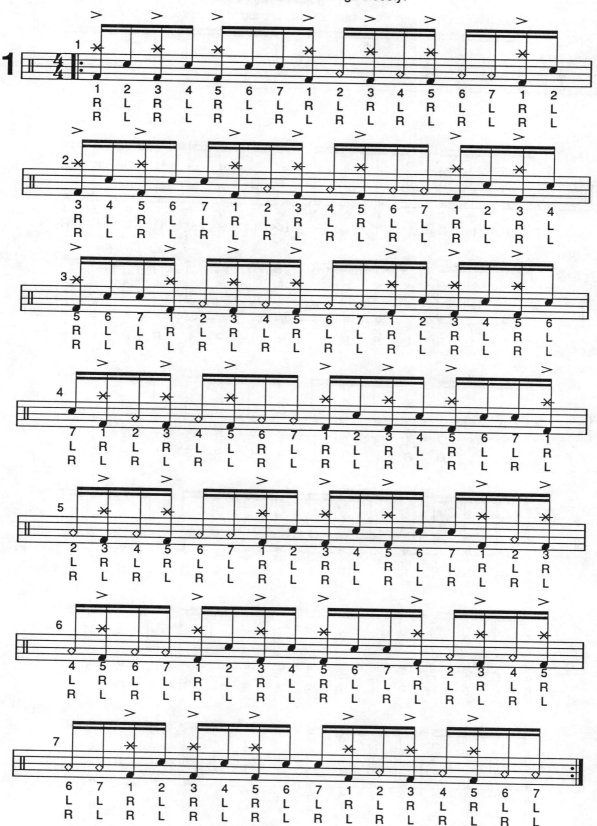

125

Applying 7/16 in 4/4 Time

This is an over the bar time exercise of 7/16 phrases in 4/4.
The backbeat or accent is on the 5th beat of the 7/16 phrase.
Practice with a quarter note click,
then break it up into 1 or 2 bar patterns preceded by 1 or 2 bars of time.

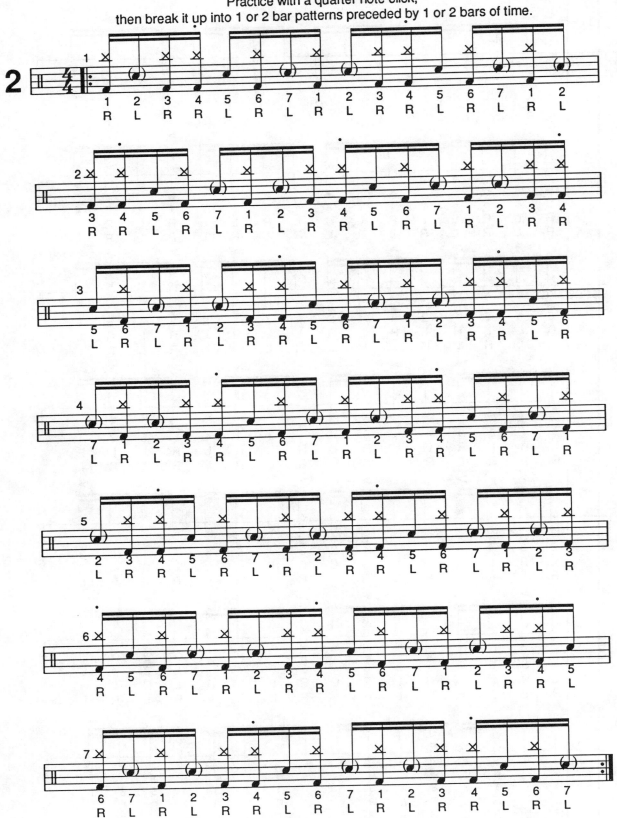

126

PolyRhythm

POLYRHYTHM - Having two or more different rhythmic pulses occurring simultaneously in an equal space of time.

THE FORMULA
To Play A against B
Multiply A times B
This is the smallest number that A and B can be divided (A X B = C)
Divide C by B
This will give you B equal groups of A (or the B pulse)
Divide C by A
This gives you the A pulse

EXAMPLE
To play 7 (A) against 4 (B)
Multiply 7 X 4 = 28 (C)
C is the total number of beats in the bar.
Write 28 equal notes in a bar.
Accenting every 7th note gives you the B pulse.
Accenting every 4th note gives you the A pulse.

* Practice the Septuplet exercises.

Septuplets

A group of 7 equal notes to be played in the time of 4 of the same kind, in the regular rhythm.
Example: 7 - 16th notes that occur in the space of a 1/4 note, or 4 16th notes in 4/4 time.
Here are some stickings and fill patterns.
Practice slowly at first until you can hear and feel the 7 subdivision.
Play 1 or 3 bars of time before each pattern.

Playing 9/16 in 4/4 Time

Follow the instructions for playing 3/16, 5/16 & 7/16 here as well.

*Play the exercises over these ostinato figures also.

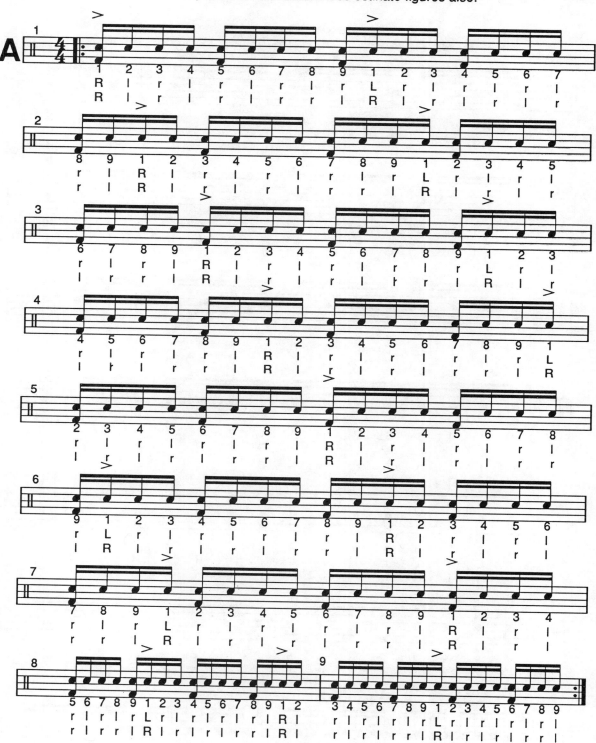

129

Playing 9/16 in 4/4 Time

Applying 9/16 in 4/4 Time

Practice the entire exercise then break it up into 1 & 2 bar patterns, preceded by 1 or 2 bars of time.

131

Applying 9/16 in 4/4 Time

Practice the entire exercise. Then break it up into 1 & 2 bar patterns. Precede with 1 or 2 bars of straight time.

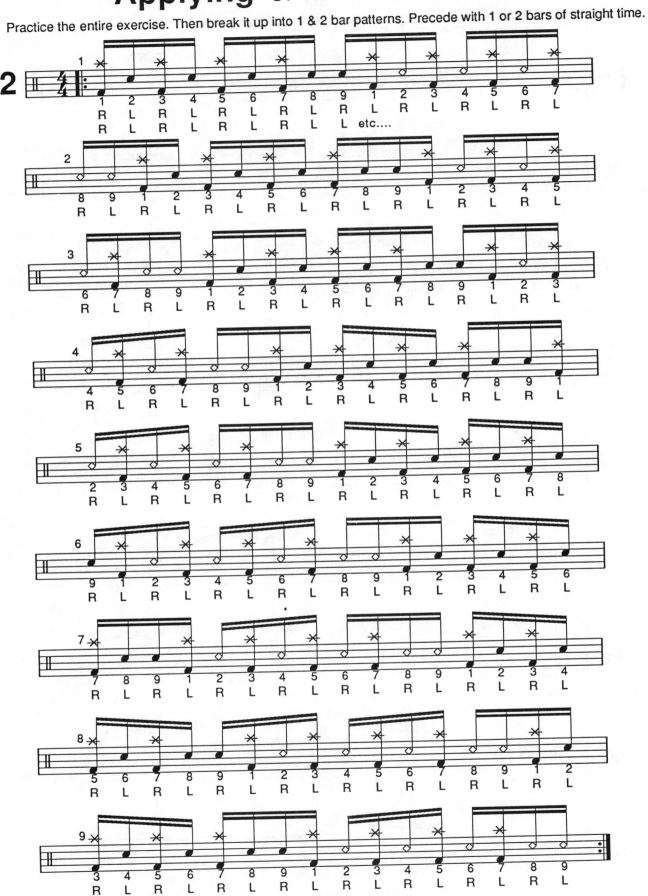

PolyRhythm

POLYRHYTHM - Having two or more different rhythmic pulses
occurring simultaneously in an equal space of time.

THE FORMULA
To Play A against B
Multiply A times B
This is the smallest number that A and B can be divided (A X B = C)
Divide C by B
This gives you the B pulse
Divide C by A
This gives you the A pulse

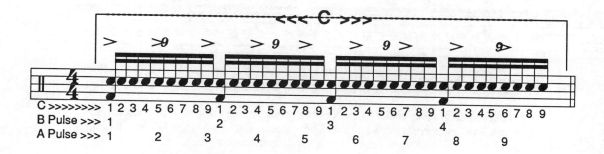

C >>>>>>>> 1 2 3 4 5 6 7 8 9 1 2 3 4 5 6 7 8 9 1 2 3 4 5 6 7 8 9 1 2 3 4 5 6 7 8 9
B Pulse >>> 1   2   3   4
A Pulse >>> 1   2   3   4   5   6   7   8   9

EXAMPLE
To play 9 (A) against 4 (B)
Multiply 9 X 4 = 36 (C)
C is the total number of beats in the bar.
Write 36 equal notes in a bar.
Accenting every 9th note will give you the B pulse.
Accenting every 4th note will give you the A pulse.

*Practice the Nonuplet exercises
and filling & soloing in a modulated rhythm.

133

Nonuplets

A group of 9 equal notes to be played in the time of 4 of the same kind, in the regular rhythm.
Example: 7 - 16th notes that occur in the space of a 1/4 note, or 4 -16th notes in 4/4 time.
Here are some stickings and fill patterns.
Practice slowly at first until you can feel and hear the 9 subdivision.
Play 1 or 3 bars of time before each pattern.

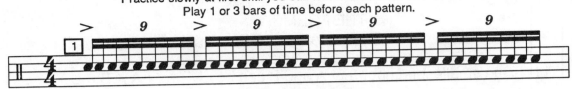

```
RLRLRLRLRLRLRLRLRLRLRLRLRLRLRLRLRLRLRL
RLRLRLRLLRLRLRLRLRLLRLRLRLRLRLLRLRLRLRLL
RLLRLLRLLRLLRLLRLLRLLRLLRLLRLLRLLRLLRLL
RLLRRRLRLLRLLRRRLRLLLRRRLRLLLRRRLRLLRRRL
```

```
RLRLRLRLRLRLRLRLRLRLRLRLRLRLRLRLRLRLRL
RLLRLLRLLRLLRLLRLLRLLRLLRLLRLLRLLRLLRLL
```

In some cases it is easier to think of the nonuplets against 1/8 note triplets.
This is not unlike playing triplets in 6/8. The accents above mark the 1/8 note triplet.
The bass drum is the 1/4 note pulse.

```
R L R L R L R L R L R L R L R L R L R L
R L L R L L R L L R L L R L L R L L R L L
```

In the pattern above the toms outline the 1/4 note triplet.
This kind of pattern works well when a 1/4 note pulse is modulated to a 1/4 triplet pulse. See "Metric Modulation".

```
R L L R R R L R . L L R R R L R L L R R L
```

Patterns 4, 5 and 6 are examples of some ordinary fill patterns superimposed over nonuplets.
Take these slow and practice with a metronome. Remember the key here is the 1/4 and 8th note triplet pulse.

134

Displacing Beats With Odd Groups

The examples on this page may be played in 16ths & 32nds also,
If necessary write them out in different note values.

Example A
A single 3-note group will move the primary accents
(1 & 3) to the & of 2 and the & of 4.
A single 5-note group will put you back on the down beat.

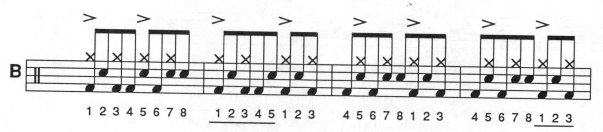

Example B
A single 5-note group will move the primary accents
(1 & 3) to the & of 1 and the & of 3.
A single 3-note group will put you back on the down beat.

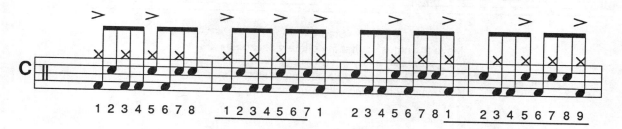

Examples C & D
Single 7 & 9-note phrases will have similar results.

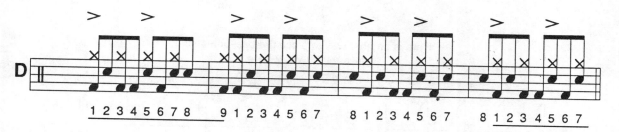

Practice these ideas with a metronome until they are comfortable
and you can HEAR how the pattern sounds flipped around.
You can use this concept with any pattern.
Experiment using it in solos and fills...

135

Superimposed Metric Modulation

Step 1.
Start with a basic pattern in duple or triple meter.

Step 2.
Subdivide into triplets

Step 3
Move the notes so that the primary backbeats are accenting every third note in the triplet. At this point your modulated pattern can be looked at as a 6/4 or 1/2 time shuffle pattern and a new foundation is in place to build on.

Step 4
Move the notes so that the primary backbeats are accenting every other note in the triplet. This gives you a cut time effect. You can play anything you would normally play in 6.

*Here is another way to place the backbeats so they stretch over 2 bars.

By filling in the rests you could superimpose any 16th note pattern. Depending on the context this could create the illusion of playing in a completely different tempo.

Superimposed Metric Modulation

Continued

Try These Patterns...

This is just a single paradiddle voiced between the kick & snare,
eighths on the hi hat.
*Note the primary accents or quarter pulse..

Same pattern modulated UP to 16th note triplets.
*Note the primary accents and the ghost strokes...

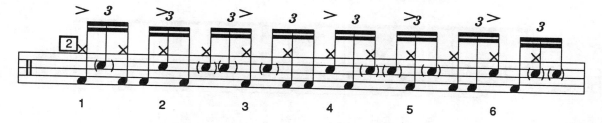

Here is another basic beat (#3). As you can see below when
it is modulated UP it becomes another animal (#4).

Practice with a metronome or drum machine.
This concept is easier to master when you practice against clock time.

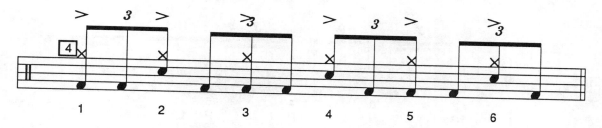

Filling & Soloing in a Modulated Time

Here are some examples of the relationship of 8th note nonuplets and 16th note triplets in a modulated rhythm. Thinking the quarter note triplet is the key. Alternate all patterns with pattern 1...

Play-Along Tape & Drum Charts

Play-Along
Drum Charts

The Music and Charts in the following section are designed to give you musical examples to practice and play along with.

Each piece covers different subject matter and relates directly to material in the preceding chapters.

The charts are basic road maps with only the most necessary information, so you may interpret them in your own style.

Sketch

This is an open piece, meaning there is a lot of space in the arrangement and it serves as an introduction to Electric.

The chord changes move in half notes leaving almost limitless rhythmic possibilities. It has a very basic AB form. I found it a perfect platform for experimenting with metric modulation, meter within meter and beat displacement. It is also fun to catch some of the melodic embellishing that occurs in the lead line.

Electric

Electric has a Latin flavor, using Baion & Songo patterns.
It also has a Montuno section to solo over.

Redd Moon

This is an odd meter piece, lots of twists, turns and hits.
Plus another Montuno in 6/4, here the solo is over a dotted eighth and sixteenth ostinato on the bass drum.

Home

This is a fusion piece in an AABA form. A more contemporary example of this song form.

Funky Track

This is a simple 12 bar form in a contemporary style. The feel is a 16th note swing.

Blues Swing

A traditional 12 bar blues form, jazz swing/mid tempo, (melody-solos-melody-end). This is a decent track to practice the patterns in the jazz section. Check out page 66 for practice tips and some suggested listening.

32 Bar

This is a more traditional 32 bar chorus form, jazz swing/uptempo (melody-melody-variation-melody) though the arrangement here picks up at the solo with an added tag ala 7 Steps to Heaven. Check out page 66 for practice tips and some suggested listening.

Listen to the tape, you can learn my approach or play it your own way.
The purpose here is help improve your reading skills and your time.

Sketch

This is a good piece of music to play just about anything you want.
Try modulations, meter within meter, beat displacement and odd note groupings etc.

Frank Briggs

*Some of the material I used for this piece can be found on pages
19, 60, 114, 116, 122, 123, 132, 135, 136 & 138.

Turn Page

Electric

Frank Briggs

<<<< **Play 16** >>>>

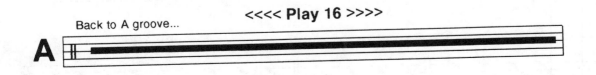

Redd Moon

Play-Along

Frank Briggs

144

Home

Frank Briggs

FunkyTrack

This track is a repeated 12 bar form in a 16th note shuffle feel.
There is more freedom than you would think in a piece of this type.
Try outlining the bass part as opposed to playing all the notes on the bass drum.
Play the triplets as loose as you can.

Frank Briggs

*Material for this piece can be found on pages
42, 47, 48 & 113.

Play-Along

Jazz Swing

Here are a couple of tracks for practicing jazz patterns
Material for these tracks can be found on pages
65, 66 & 67-71.

12 Bar Blues Form

32 Bar
32 Bar Chorus Form

Appendix

PRACTICE SUGGESTIONS

TIME...
Practice all material at different tempos with a metronome, drum machine or sequencer.

DYNAMICS...
Distance equals volume. Practice all material at different stick heights.

TAPE YOURSELF...
Listen for feel, tendency to rush or drag, creativity, taste, balance, etc.

EXPERIMENT...
Be creative! Once you have learned an exercise, use the creative techniques like beat displacement or metric modulation, to come up with new ideas.

GET ORGANIZED...
Organize your study materials. I have a brief case just for that purpose. I keep a portable tape recorder, a metronome (I recommend the Dr. Beat made by Boss) and a 3 ring binder with manuscript paper for jotting down ideas. Keep a file of your new ideas. This is a great way to develop & retain your own vocabulary.

GENERAL ADVICE

ATTITUDE...
Try at all times to be positive and professional. A great attitude will get you farther than you may think.

EQUIPMENT...
The general rule here is, make sure everything works, sounds good, and looks decent. It is all part of being a professional.

BIG EARS...
Listen to what is being played around you and how you are locking with the other musicians. Play in context and make the other musicians sound good and you will sound good as well.

CONFIDENCE verses EGO...
Knowing the music and your parts will give you confidence in your ability to handle the demands of your situation. Let your music speak for itself.

INSPIRATION...
Try to be one...

PATIENCE...
Some things take time, be patient. Some of the lessons in this book are very challenging and will not be mastered in a single day, take your time.

Suggested Listening

Album	Artist	Drummer
Light as a Feather	Chick Corea	Airto
On The Corner	John Patitucci	Al Foster, Colaiuta, Weckl
Greatest Hits	Booker T. & the MG's	Al Jackson
Heavy Weather	Weather Report	Alex Acuna
Fresh	Sly & The Family Stone	Andy Newmark
A Night At BirdLand	Art Blakey	Art Blakey
Keystone 3	Art Blakey	Art Blakey
New Pants	Flim & The BB's	Bill Berg
One of a Kind	Bruford	Bill Bruford
The Beat	King Crimson	Bill Bruford
Spectrum	Billy Cobham	Billy Cobham
Total Eclipse	Billy Cobham	Billy Cobham
Between Nothingness & Eternity	Mahavishnu Orchestra	Billy Cobham
Inner Mounting Flame	Mahavishnu Orchestra	Billy Cobham
Jack Johnson	Miles Davis	Billy Cobham
Blood, Sweat & Tears	Blood, Sweat, & Tears	Bobby Columby
Tchokola	Jon Luc Ponty	Brice Wassy
Big Swing Face	Buddy Rich	Buddy Rich
West Side Story	Buddy Rich	Buddy Rich
Rich Verses Roach	Buddy Rich / Max Roach	Buddy Rich / Max Roach
Metal Fatigue	Allan Holdsworth	Chad Wackerman
Live	Dire Straights	Chris Whitten
On The Other Hand	Michel Camillo	Cliff Almond
The Best of James Brown	James Brown	Clyde Stubblefield,Various
Aquamarine	Dan Gottlieb	Dan Gottlieb
Blown Away	Elements	Dan Gottlieb
Akoustic Band Live	Chick Corea	Dave Weckl
Elektric Band	Chick Corea	Dave Weckl
Master Plan	Dave Weckl	Dave Weckl
On Fire	Michel Camilo	Dave Weckl
Back To Oakland	Tower of Power	David Garibaldi
Getting Even	Dennis Chambers	Dennis Chambers
Pick Hits Live	John Scofield	Dennis Chambers
The Night Fly	Donald Fagen	Ed Green
Aja	Steely Dan	Ed Green
Doc Severenson Live	Doc Severenson	Ed Shaughnessy
A Love Supreme	John Coltrane	Elvin Jones
Speak No Evil	Wayne Shorter	Elvin Jones
Live in Montreal	Gino Vannelli	Enzo Todesco
Stand in Line	805	Frank Briggs
Greatest Hits	Earth Wind & Fire	Fred White
Metal Fatigue	Allan Holdsworth	Gary Husband
"Sing,Sing,Sing,"	Benny Goodman	Gene Krupa
Disraeli Gears	Creem	Ginger Baker
Siblings	Greg Bissonette	Greg Bissonette
Head Hunters	Herbie Hancock	Harvey Mason
Earth Walk	Jack DeJohnette	Jack DeJohnette
80/81	Pat Metheny	Jack Dejohnette
Silk Degrees	Boz Skaggs	Jeff Porcaro
The NightFly	Donald Fagen	Jeff Porcaro
Another Time... Another Place	Sandi Patti	Jeff Porcaro
Toto IV	Toto	Jeff Porcaro
Think Of One	Wynton Marsalis	Jeff Watts
Security	Peter Gabriel	Jerry Morrata
Layla	Derick & The Dominos	Jim Gordon
Clip Joint Rhumba	Ry Cooder	Jim Keltner
Time Out	Dave Brubeck	Joe Morello
Celebration	Paquito D Revera	Joel Rosenblatt

Suggested Listening

Album	Artist	Drummer
Live at Sweet Basil	Randy Brecker	Joey Baron
Box Set	Led Zeppelin	John Bonham
Led Zeppelin	Led Zeppelin	John Bonham
Tommy	The Who	Keith Moon
JB Horns	Maceo Parker	Kenwood Dennard
Romantic Warrior	Chick Corea	Lenny White
Any	Return To Forever	Lenny White
Random Abstract	Branford Marsalis	Lewis Nash
Ellington Uptown	Duke Ellington	Louie Bellson
The Soul Cages	Sting	Manu Katche
Brother to Brother	Gino Vannelli	Mark Craney
Deeds Not Words	Max Roach	Max Roach
Nearly Human	Todd Rundgren	Michael Urbano
Vision of the Emerald Beyond	Mahavishnu Orchestra	Michael Waldon
The Green Album	Eddie Jobson	Mike Barsimonto
Freedom to Fly	Tony MacAlpine	Mike Terrana
Are You Experienced	Jimi Hendricks	Mitch Mitchell
Go On	Mr. Mister	Pat Mastelotto
Untitled	The Rembrandts	Pat Mastelotto
Aja	Steely Dan	Paul Humphrey
8:30	Weather Report	Peter Erskine
Face Value	Phil Collins	Phil Collins
Running In The Family	Level 42	Phil Gould
Milestones	Miles Davis	Philly Joe Jones
The Royal Scam	Steely Dan	Rick Moratta, Bernard Purdie
Touch the World	Earth Wind & Fire	Rickie Lawson
Sgt. Peppers	The Beatles	Ringo Starr
Waiting for Columbus	Little Feat	Ritchie Hayward
Divided We Stand	The Dregs	Rod Morganstein
Now He Sings ..Now He Sobs	Chick Corea	Roy Haynes
Breakfast Wine	Bobby Shew	Sherman Ferguson
There & Back	Jeff Beck	Simon Phillips
Greatest Hits	Average White Band	Steve Ferrone
Three Quartets	Chick Corea	Steve Gadd
Aja	Steely Dan	Steve Gadd, Bernard Purdie
Blades	Steve Khan	Steve Jordan
Dancing on the Edge of the World	Kit Walker	Steve Smith
Vita Live	Vital Information	Steve Smith
Ghost In The Machine	The Police	Stewart Copeland
Zenyatta Mondatta	The Police	Stewart Copeland
Gamalon	Gamalon	Ted Reinhart
Guitar Shop	Jeff Beck	Terry Bozzio
Heavy Metal Bebop	The Brecker Brothers	Terry Bozzio
Tap Step	Chick Corea	Tom Brechtlein
Robben Ford & The Blue Line	Robben Ford & The Blue Line	Tom Brechtlein
Ah Via Musicom	Eric Johnson	Tommy Taylor
Quartet	Herbie Hancock	Tony Williams
Miles Smiles	Miles Davis	Tony Williams
Believe It	The New Tony Williams Lifetime	Tony Williams
Spring	Tony Williams	Tony Williams
Hat	Mike Keneally	Toss Panos
Live at The Royal Festival Hall	John McLaughlin	Trilok Gurtu
Joe's Garage	Frank Zappa	Vinnie Calaiuta
Works	Nik Kershaw	Vinnie Colaiuta
10 Sumner's Tales	Sting	Vinnie Colaiuta
Vivid	Living Colour	Will Calhoun
Four Corners	The Yellow Jackets	Will Kennedy
Rejuvenation	The Meters	Ziggy Modeleste

Glossary

Notes & Rests

NOTE
A character that represents the duration of rhythmic sound.
REST
A character that represents the duration of silence.
Each note has an equivalent rest.

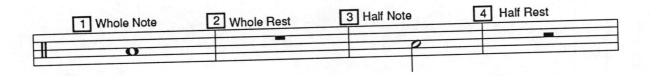

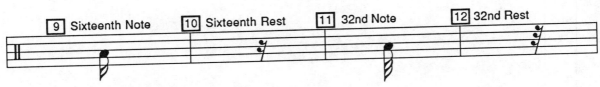

DOTTED NOTES & RESTS
A dot placed after a note or rest increases the duration of that note or rest by 1/2...
EX: a dotted 8th note is equal in space to an 8th and one 16th.

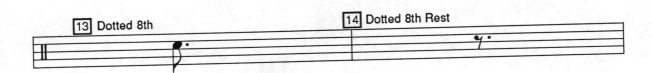

DOUBLE DOTTED NOTES & RESTS
2 dots after a note or rest increases the duration by 3/4...
EX. a double dotted quarter is equal in space to a quarter and 3 16th notes.

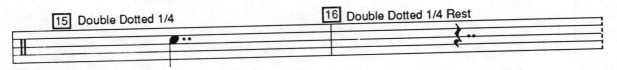

Signs & Marks

FERMATA (HOLD)
This sign placed over a note or rest means that the note or rest is to be held beyond it's normal value.

ACCENT
A note with this sign over it is to be played with more emphasis or louder (accented)

TIE
A curved line connecting 2 notes of the same pitch. The second note is not played, it's duration is added to that of the first note.

TIME SIGNATURE
The top number is the number of beats in the measure. The bottom number is the note value that receives one beat.

COMMON TIME
Same as 4/4 time.

CUT TIME
Also called double time. A quarter note becomes a half note.

Simile
in the style or spirit of... (SIMILE)

(or any number) an abbreviation
Play time for 8 bars
PLAY 8

CRESCENDO
Increasing in volume.

DECRESCENDO
Decreasing in volume.

DAL SEGNO
or DS sign
The sign you return to in a DS.

CODA
This is another sign usually used in conjunction with a DS or DC to notate a repeat of a particular part in a piece of music.
EX. DS to coda or beginning to coda.

REPEAT SIGN
This sign means repeat the previous measure.

REPEAT SIGN
This sign means repeat the previous 2 measures.
2

REPEAT MARKS
A pair of double dotted bars means that the music between these marks is to be repeated once.

155

Signs & Marks

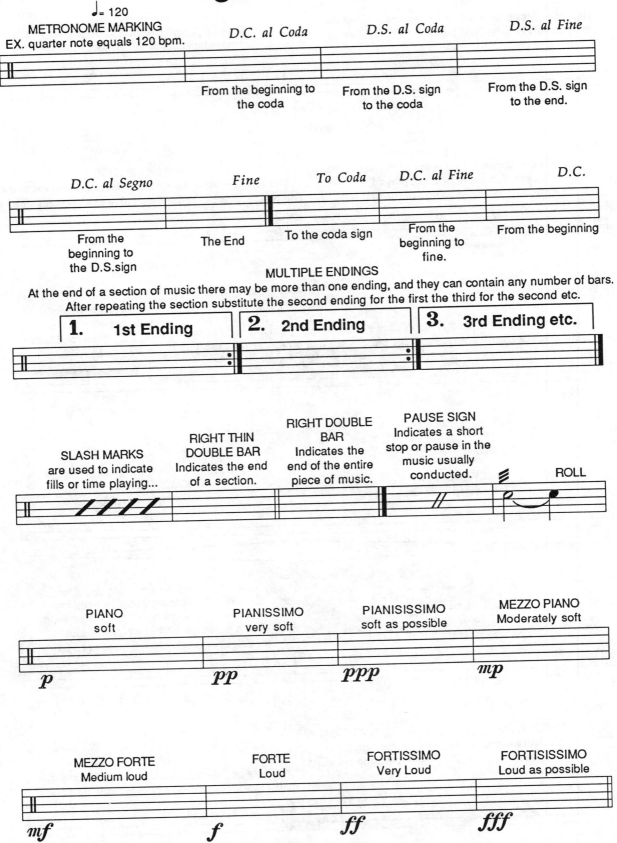

♩= 120
METRONOME MARKING
EX. quarter note equals 120 bpm.

D.C. al Coda

D.S. al Coda

D.S. al Fine

From the beginning to
the coda

From the D.S. sign
to the coda

From the D.S. sign
to the end.

D.C. al Segno

Fine

To Coda

D.C. al Fine

D.C.

From the
beginning to
the D.S.sign

The End

To the coda sign

From the
beginning to
fine.

From the beginning

MULTIPLE ENDINGS

At the end of a section of music there may be more than one ending, and they can contain any number of bars.
After repeating the section substitute the second ending for the first the third for the second etc.

1.   1st Ending

2.   2nd Ending

3.   3rd Ending etc.

SLASH MARKS
are used to indicate
fills or time playing...

RIGHT THIN
DOUBLE BAR
Indicates the end
of a section.

RIGHT DOUBLE
BAR
Indicates the
end of the entire
piece of music.

PAUSE SIGN
Indicates a short
stop or pause in the
music usually
conducted.

ROLL

PIANO
soft

PIANISSIMO
very soft

PIANISISSIMO
soft as possible

MEZZO PIANO
Moderately soft

p

pp

ppp

mp

MEZZO FORTE
Medium loud

FORTE
Loud

FORTISSIMO
Very Loud

FORTISISSIMO
Loud as possible

mf

f

ff

fff

156

TIME

1. Same as tempo
2. The division of the measure into equal fractional parts of a whole note,
forming a standard for the accentuation or regular rhythmic flow of the music.

THERE ARE TWO CLASSES OF TIME
DUPLE & TRIPLE
In DUPLE time or meter the number of beats to the measure is divisible by two.
In TRIPLE time or meter the number of beats to the measure is divisible by three.

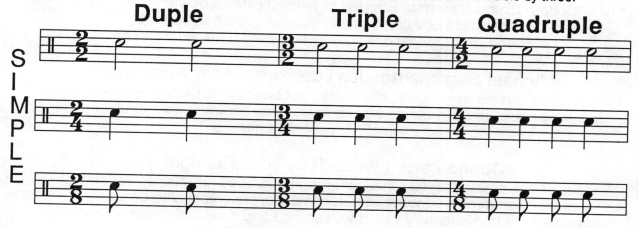

THERE ARE ALSO TWO SUB CLASSES
COMPOUND DUPLE TIME & COMPOUND TRIPLE TIME

IN COMPOUND DUPLE TIME
the number of beats to a bar is still divisible by two,
but each beat contains instead of an ordinary note divisible by 2,
a dotted note (or it's equivalent in other notes and rests) divisible by 3:
hence the term compound.

IN COMPOUND TRIPLE TIME
not only is the number of beats in each measure divisible by three but also each beat.

TIME FEEL
When you hear someone refer to a drummer as having good time, what they are referring to is
his or her ability to make the music feel good while keeping the tempo steady.

157

"MODERN DRUMSET "By Frank Briggs
Book & Play-along Cassette
RECOMMENDED BY THESE FINE ARTISTS...

Chad Wackerman (Solo Artist / Allan Holdsworth / Frank Zappa)
"Frank has written a book that covers the full spectrum of drumming, from the basics to some very advanced polyrhythmic concepts. I recommend it to any serious drummer."

Ed Shaughnessy (Tonight Show Band / Count Basie)
"Modern Drumset Method is a well organized system of written and aural material to develop drumset skills, a great book & tape package...congratulations, I know how hard book work can be"

Michael Barsimanto (Jon Luc-Ponty / Andy Summers)
"Everything in here is solid information not busy work. Once you see and feel the shapes of the patterns and exercises you naturally want to invent your own course... This book is <u>musical</u>."

Doane Perry (Jethro Tull / Todd Rundgren)
"Frank has created an extremely thorough and comprehensive overview of modern drumming concepts and techniques, encompassing every style imaginable. A tremendously valuable resource and a valuable method book for drummers and teachers alike"...

Bob Gatzen (Product Designer / Composer)
"This type of book is timeless, like Stone's "Stick Control" or Reed's "Syncopation". It is an encyclopedia for the drumset"...

Toss Panos (Steve Vai / Dweezil Zappa / Fire Merchants)
"As far as books are concerned I think Modern Drumset Method is the logical next step from Joe Porcaro's Drumset Method, and the play-along tape is !!#?&!* Smoking!"

Mark Sanders (Jackson 5 / Tower of Power)
"Frank's book Modern Drumset...is just that. Modern concepts for drummers who want to push the envelope of drumming ...and the tape is slamming."

Cliff Almond (Michel Camillo / John Pattitucci)
"This is a great piece of work.
I let a friend of mine borrow it and now I can't get it back."

Glen Sobel (Tony MacAlpine, P.I.T. Instructor)
"Frank pulls out all the stops with Modern Drumset Method. The lessons are clearly articulated and intelligent, and the play-along tape jams...Makes a great teaching companion"

Also...

Mike Terrana (Yngwie Malmstein) **Tony Braunagel** (Bonnie Raitt / Rickie Lee Jones)
David Northrup (Les Dudek) **Sherman Ferguson** (Kenney Burrell)
Matt Sorum (Guns & Roses) **David Olson** (Robert Cray) **Tom Allen** (Robin Beck, Paul Young)
Tony Verderosa (Clinician / Solo Artist) **Pamela Antonino** (Angela Bofill)